Que's
Guide to XTree ®

BRIAN UNDERDAHL

CREDITS

Publisher
Lloyd J. Short

Product Director
Shelley O'Hara

Production Editor
Cindy Morrow

Technical Editor
Lynette Nichols-Healey

Production Team
Claudia Bell, Michelle Cleary, Mark Enochs,
Brook Farling, Audra Hershman, Bob LaRoche,
Linda Seifert, John Sleeva, Bruce Steed, Suzanne
Tully, Allan Wimmer, Phil Worthington,
Christine Young

Trademark Acknowledgments

1-2-3 and Lotus are registered trademarks of Lotus Development
Corporation.

AutoCAD is a registered trademark of Autodesk, Inc.

dBASE is a registered trademark of Ashton-Tate Corporation.

Macintosh is a registered trademark of Apple Computer, Inc.

Microsoft Windows and MS-DOS are registered trademarks of
Microsoft Corporation.

The Norton Utilities is a registered trademark of Symantec
Corporation.

WordPerfect is a registered trademark of WordPerfect Corporation.
XTree is a registered trademark and XTree Easy and XTree Gold
are trademarks of Executive Systems, Inc.

To Dawn, Keith, and Christa. May all your futures be bright.

ABOUT THE AUTHOR

Brian Underdahl

Brian Underdahl is an independent consultant based in Reno, Nevada. He is the author of the best-selling *Upgrading to MS-DOS 5* (Que Corporation), as well as a large number of other books from several major computer book publishers. He was the technical editor of *Using 1-2-3, Release 2.3*; *Computerizing Your Small Business*; and many other fine books from Que Corporation. His background in engineering and business give him the ability to present complex subjects in a clear and concise manner.

CONTENTS AT A GLANCE

TABLE OF CONTENTS

INTRODUCTION

Que's Guide to XTree offers a new approach to a very popular program—XTree. It shows you how to use XTree and explains in clear, simple language how the often-confusing mix of XTree commands work together to help you manage your files and directories. In addition, you will learn how to create and modify the XTree application menu so that you can use XTree as a menu for running all your DOS programs.

This book concentrates on the most recent versions of XTree—XTreeGold 2.0 and 2.5 and XTree Easy. You will not find a confusing mix of old and new commands. Instead, you will find a clear guide to making XTree work for you.

XTree has many features and can be difficult to master. Some users never use XTree as more than an application menu and others use it only to manage files. Regardless of your XTree experience, *Que's Guide to XTree* will help you become a more efficient XTree user.

Introducing XTree

X Tree is a software program for the IBM-PC and compatible systems that fits into a category loosely known as a "utility" program. That is, it has many functions, but is not a primary application, such as a word processor like WordPerfect, a database manager like dBASE, or a spreadsheet program like Lotus 1-2-3.

Utility programs come in many flavors. Some are used primarily to recover from hard disk disasters and operator's errors. Others, like PKZIP, compress files into organized libraries. XTree includes many of the same functions and adds many more features, including file management and a DOS Shell that enables you to run application programs from a simple-to-use menu.

The following sections present an overview of XTree's features. Later chapters show you how to use XTree effectively.

XTree as a File Manager

Managing the files on your computer's hard disk can be frustrating and confusing. DOS is a command line-oriented operating system, as opposed to a graphically oriented one, such as the Windows environment or the Macintosh System. Unless you spend considerable time learning the DOS commands, remembering exactly which command you need to use is difficult at best.

XTree takes a different approach to managing your files. Instead of hard-to-remember commands, XTree gives you a graphical view of your hard disk directory structure and the files on the disk. You simply point to directories or files instead of trying to remember their names and locations. Figure 1.1 shows a typical XTree screen.

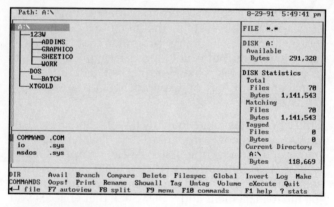

Fig. 1.1. The XTree screen.

Managing Individual Files

The simplest and most straightforward file management activities involve individual files. You will probably, for example, want to copy a single data file from
your hard disk to a floppy disk fairly often.

Suppose that your database records are contained in
a directory named DATA, which is under the program
directory DBMANAGE on your C drive. To copy a
database file called CONTACTS.DBF to a diskette in
the A: drive, you would use one of several different
DOS commands.

Although the commands are not too difficult to remember after you learn them, remembering the exact
syntax of the commands and knowing when you need
one instead of another can be confusing. Weren't
computers supposed to make life easier? Why should
you have to be frustrated by such a simple task?

XTree was designed to make these simple file management chores easier. You no longer have to remember complicated commands. With XTree, you can
copy a file by highlighting the file on-screen, selecting
a command from a menu, and answering a few
prompts. (Chapter 4 covers the steps in detail.)

Likewise, XTree also makes other file-management
tasks easier, such as moving files from one place to
another; removing old, obsolete files; (in many cases)
recovering files you have erased accidentally;
changing file names; and editing files (such as
AUTOEXEC.BAT and CONFIG.SYS—two special files
that are used to customize the operation of your PC).

Managing Groups of Files

Although you most often work on a single file at a time, you occasionally must manage a group of related files.

DOS enables you to specify multiple files using what are called *wild cards*. Using wild cards, however, can be complicated. The two wild cards DOS allows are the asterisk (*) and the question mark (?). The asterisk matches all remaining characters in either the file name or the extension, and the question mark matches a single character.

NOTE A question mark wild card that is not followed by another character matches both a single character and no characters. On the other hand, following question mark wild cards with another character requires that each question mark be replaced by exactly one character, or the names will not match.

Although wild cards enable you to work with groups of files when the files have similar names, they do not help when files have dissimilar names or when the files you want have similar names to other files. In the following group of files, for example, you could not use wild cards effectively to select some—but not all—files with 1992 as the last four characters:

ACCT1992.WK1

BENS1992.WK1

CONS1992.WK1

DEBT1992.WK1

GENL1992.WK1

RENO1992.WK1

WORK1992.WK1

In a situation such as this, copying ACCT1992.WK1, BENS1992.WK1, and DEBT1992.WK1 without copying CONS1992.WK1, GENL1992.WK1, RENO1992.WK1, and WORK1992.WK1 would require three different DOS commands.

XTree, on the other hand, enables you to select each of the files you want to copy, and then issue a single copy command. In fact, if all the files selected will not fit on a single disk, XTree even lets you interrupt the copy, format additional disks if necessary, and continue from the point of interruption. Using DOS commands, you would have to reissue the copy commands and hope that you remembered where you had left off.

XTree also enables you to move, delete, and rename groups of files with a single command. In fact, XTree only limits you to working on one file at a time when you are editing files. Even then, however, you can select a group of files for editing, although you make changes to one file at a time. In Chapter 4, "Managing Files," you will learn how to use XTree to perform file management functions.

Managing Directories

The DOS directory structure is often called a tree-structured directory; hence the name XTree for a utility program designed to help you manage files. Whether or not you add directories to a disk, all DOS disks have at least one directory—the "root" directory.

Directories help you organize your files into logical groups. You might want to place your word process-ing program files in a separate directory. You then can place your documents in subdirectories of the word processing program directory. Likewise, your spreadsheet program can be in its own directory with subdirectories for different types of worksheet files.

Usually, all DOS files are also stored in their own directory—often this directory is called C:\DOS.

> **NOTE** The root directory is the lowest directory on a disk. All other directories start at the root directory and build outwards. The root directory, however, does not have the name ROOT. Instead you refer to the root directory by using a backslash (\). The root directory on the C: drive, for example, is referred to using C:\. To avoid confusion, do not create a directory called ROOT.

Not only do directories make logical sense, they also are practical. If you want to back up your word processing documents, you do not need to copy the word processing program files, all the DOS files, the spreadsheet program, and your worksheets. Although XTree makes processing groups of files much easier, you will find that a sensible directory structure that separates files by function makes using XTree even more efficient.

All directories below the root directory are a special type of DOS file. In spite of this fact, many operations that you can perform easily on normal files are difficult or impossible using DOS commands. For example, you cannot change the name of a directory.

Copying a directory structure is also difficult using DOS commands. XTree also makes this task quite simple.

Navigating through a tree-structured directory can be frustrating. Refer back to figure 1.1. You see a disk with many directories.

If you want to move from A:\123W to
A:\123W\WORK, you can simply enter

CD WORK <Enter>

If, on the other hand, you want to move from A:\DOS
to A:\123W\WORK, you must enter

CD \123W\WORK <Enter>

Using XTree makes navigating your directories a
snap. Figure 1.2 shows the XTree screen when ·
A:\123W\WORK is the current directory. Figure 1.3
shows what happens when you press ↓—A:\DOS
becomes the current directory with a single key
press.

```
Path: A:\123W\WORK                         8-29-91  6:13:11 pm

A:\                                   │ FILE  *.*
  ├─123W                              │
  │   ├─ADDINS                        │ DISK  A:
  │   ├─GRAPHICO                      │ Available
  │   ├─SHEETICO                      │   Bytes     225,280
  │   └─WORK                          │
  ├─DOS                              │ DISK Statistics
  │   └─BATCH                         │ Total
  └─XTGOLD                           │   Files          85
                                      │   Bytes   1,202,768
                                      │ Matching
                                      │   Files          85
                                      │   Bytes   1,202,768
                                      │ Tagged
                                      │   Files           0
  3DAREA  .WK3    CACTUS  .WK3   FREQUENC.WK3 │   Bytes           0
  3DBAR   .WK3    CARDLIST.WK3   FUNCTION.WK3 │ Current Directory
  AUDITREE.WK3    CARDS   .WK3   LEDGER  .WK3 │   WORK
  BACKTREE.WK3    FREQTYPE.WK3   SCANTYPE.WK3 │   Bytes      61,225

DIR       Avail  Branch  Compare  Delete  Filespec  Global  Invert  Log  Make
COMMANDS  Oops!  Print  Rename  Showall  Tag  Untag  Volume  eXecute  Quit
←┘ file   F7 autoview   F8 split    F9 menu  F10 commands   F1 help  < > select
```

Fig. 1.2. XTree showing A:\123W\WORK as the current directory.

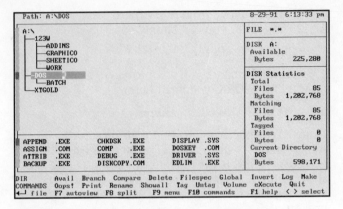

Fig. 1.3. Pressing ↓ once makes A:\DOS the current directory.

Chapter 6 shows you how to use XTree to navigate directories, as well as to create, rename, display, and print them.

XTree as an Application Menu Generator

XTree has another major function—one that, for many users, is just as important as its file management capabilities. With XTree, you can set up an application menu and run your programs by simply selecting the programs from a list.

Automating Program Startup

When you install XTree, you can have XTree search for programs on your hard disk and automatically add them to a menu. You also can, if you prefer, create your own XTree application menu later. Regardless of the method used, the menu lets you

execute other programs—not related to XTree—
without entering the often-complex series of
commands necessary to start a program.

Figure 1.4 shows a typical XTree application menu
that includes several categories of programs. The
first group, BUSINESS, contains five different business
programs that you can run simply by highlighting the
desired program and pressing Enter. You can easily
select other groups in the same manner, and the
effect is the same—the steps required to execute
the program are performed automatically.

In addition to using XTree application menus to make
starting programs on your PC easier, you also can
create menus that enable other users to select programs without the bother of learning the DOS commands.

Fig. 1.4. An XTree application menu.

Making Your PC Easier To Use

You aren't limited to including computer programs
on XTree's application menus. XTree only includes

such programs when it generates a menu, but you can also add other options that make your PC even easier to use.

You also can tie items on XTree application menus to command scripts that perform other tasks, such as formatting a disk or backing up files. You could, for example, have one menu option to format low-density disks in your A drive, and another to format high-density disks in the same drive. Chapter 7 describes XTree application menus in detail.

Summary

This chapter provided a brief overview of XTree's capabilities. It gave you a glimpse at file management and showed you how XTree can work with individual files, groups of files, and directories. You also learned a little about XTree application menus. Later chapters expand greatly on these subjects and show you how to use XTree effectively.

Chapter 2 examines the many different versions of XTree and explains which versions this book covers.

Understanding XTree's Many Versions

One problem with trying to cover a program such as XTree in a compact, easy-to-use book is that so many different versions of the program have emerged since its introduction in 1985. With the new XTree Gold 2.5 release, there have been seven major releases, plus many minor, maintenance releases.

This book concentrates on the currently available XTree versions. The book contains a straightforward approach that explains exactly what you need to know—how to use XTree's current versions effectively.

Owners of older XTree versions should take heart, however; Appendix B is a cross-reference to the other versions of XTree. In addition, you will find that most procedures are similar in all versions of the program. Except for features added in later program versions, owners of older releases of XTree will find only minor command procedure changes and should easily be able to adapt the tasks in this book to their version.

The following sections provide an overview of the
different versions of XTree.

XTreeGold 2.0 and 2.5

XTreeGold 2.0 and the newly released XTreeGold 2.5
are the most advanced versions of XTree. The following sections describe the new features of XTreeGold.

New Pull-Down Menus

The pull-down menus added to XTreeGold let you
access all XTree commands in sensible, organized
groups. Using the pull-down menus is usually much
easier than trying to remember the functions of the
different command groups at the bottom of the
screen. Also, because the pull-down menus work particularly well with a mouse, XTreeGold is even easier
for mouse owners to use. Figure 2.1 shows one of the
XTreeGold pull-down menus.

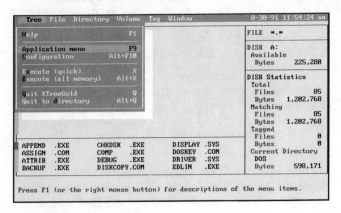

Fig. 2.1. XTreeGold includes easy-to-use pull-down menus.

Native Format File Viewers

Both XTreeGold 2.0 and XTreeGold 2.5 can view many types of files in their native format—as the files would appear in the program that created the file. The primary difference between XTreeGold 2.0 and XTreeGold 2.5, however, is the addition of graphics file viewers in Release 2.5. In addition to the spread-sheet, database, word processor, and archive file format viewers of Release 2.0, Release 2.5 can display a large variety of graphics files (such as PCX, AutoCAD, and TIFF files) exactly as they would appear in the program that created the file.

Automatic Building of Application Menus

Building an application menu automatically when you install XTreeGold is another feature of XTreeGold. In previous releases, you had to create the application menu yourself; these current versions, however, make the process easier. Simply answer a prompt when you're installing XTree, and the menu is built for you automatically. XTreeGold searches your hard disk for programs from its list of over one thousand programs. It then adds to your application menu any programs it finds on your hard disk that are contained on its list. It also adds the commands that are necessary to execute the program.

XTreeGold also lets you add more menu items than earlier XTree versions let you add. You then can easily collapse the menu to show only the main groups, and you also can expand only the individual branches that you want.

Support for ZIP Archive File Format

XTreeGold also supports file archiving. Archiving reduces the size of most files and creates library files that can contain several files in a single file.

XTreeGold now uses the more popular ZIP format, instead of the older ARC format, as the default when compressing and archiving files. Because XTreeGold uses the ZIP format, you can exchange files with other PC users who do not have XTree, provided that they have the widely available PKZIP and PKUNZIP programs. Also, because the ZIP format usually results in greater compression than the ARC format, your archive files are smaller—taking even less disk space or time to transmit.

In addition, XTreeGold includes a program, ARC2ZIP.EXE, that converts the older ARC format files to the newer ZIP format.

Automatic File Comparisons

XTreeGold can now automatically seek out and compare files with the same names, regardless of their location on your hard disk. XTreeGold can easily find all the copies of a file, show you the newest one, and help you free the space wasted by the older, obsolete versions of the file.

Move Files in a Single Step

Earlier versions of XTree enabled you to move files between two locations on a single disk. XTreeGold, however, goes a step further by enabling you to move files from one disk to another in a single step.

One good use for this new capability is to move old files from your hard disk onto diskettes for permanent storage. Also, you can combine these two capabilities (finding older versions of files with the same name elsewhere on your disk and moving files from one disk to another) to clean out old files quickly, while still keeping them for future reference.

Two other options you might consider instead of moving files from one disk to another are using the DOS BACKUP command and using XTreeGold's archiving functions. Deciding which method to use depends on your needs. Chapter 4 provides detailed information about moving files, and Chapter 5 covers archiving.

Recovery of Accidentally Deleted Files

The final major enhancement offered in XTreeGold is the Oops! command, which recovers files that you deleted accidentally. Chapter 4 tells you how to use the Oops! command and explains a little about how it works its magic.

These sections have covered only the newest features included in XTreeGold. Chapter 1 covered the general range of XTree functions—all of which are also included in XTreeGold. The following sections provide a short view of the differences between XTreeGold and the other programs that fit under the XTree umbrella.

XTree Easy

As you might imagine, XTree Easy is intended to be a down-scaled, easy-to-use version of XTreeGold. It is, however, much improved compared to the original

XTree, and it is much closer to XTreeGold. XTree
Easy shares many features with XTreeGold, including

- Pull-down menus for commands

- Building application menus automatically

- Greater latitude in the number of menu items

- Moving files from one disk to another in a single
  step

XTree Easy uses the same commands as XTreeGold
to perform those functions that are shared by the two
programs. You will find XTree Easy both powerful
and easy-to-use.

XTree Easy does not include all the features of
XTreeGold, of course. The primary functions it lacks
are ones that potentially could be dangerous if used
incorrectly, such as Prune and Graft; it also doesn't
include Compare, Oops!, and the native format file
viewers.

XTree Net

XTree Net is basically XTreeGold with a few added
features that make it capable of working successfully
in a network environment. Most of these features
relate to remote resources—other PCs on the network and hard disks that are not directly installed in
your PC.

Networks enable many different users to share
common resources. As useful as this type of access
sounds, however, it does come with a price.

Suppose that two people were trying to update the
same record at the same time. Although both might
have a legitimate reason to update the original
record, changes made by one person might affect the
changes made by the other. Controls are necessary to
prevent conflicting changes, and the network provides these controls.

Networks also have other types of necessary controls, such as restricting access to certain files.

XTree Net recognizes the need to apply network controls. It also has an additional feature that enables one user to assist another by letting one PC take total control of another PC on the network. With this capability, a user-support person can help another user on the network without physically moving to the second person's PC.

XTree Net uses the same commands as XTreeGold for the features they share.

Older XTree Versions

The original XTree, released on April 1, 1985, offered a new level of convenience for the PC user, and each version since has added many new features.

Selecting the versions of XTree that this book should cover was complicated by the many older versions of XTree still in use. In the end, however, the decision was not too difficult. Although a substantial number of XTree users are still using older program versions, newer XTree users will likely need more help learning to be productive with XTree, and newer users will probably be using XTreeGold or XTree Easy.

If you are using an older version of XTree and you sent in your registration card when you purchased XTree, you can upgrade to XTreeGold 2.5 for $39.95 ($19.95 for owners of XTreeGold 2.0). For further information, call or write

> XTree Company
> 4330 Santa Fe Road
> San Luis Obispo,California 93401
> (805) 541-0604

Summary

Although XTree has had many major and minor revisions since its introduction in 1985, many features are shared throughout the versions. The balance of this book concentrates on the current versions, but users of older XTree versions will still find much useful information. In most cases, XTreeGold retains the same commands that were used in earlier versions, and the text shows alternative methods for performing many tasks. For more complete information on the differences between XTreeGold and older XTree versions, see Appendix B.

Learning XTree Basics

X Tree looks different than the standard DOS screen, and it can be somewhat confusing the first time you load the program. In this chapter, you will learn how to start XTree and how to understand and use XTree's many different screens—including the on-line help screens. After you understand XTree's screens, using XTree will be much easier.

If you haven't installed XTree yet, turn to Appendix A. After you install the program, return to this chapter.

Starting XTree

Starting XTree is easy, but by understanding a few basic DOS concepts, you can make the process even easier.

Starting XTree from the DOS Prompt

If you asked the XTree installation program to modify your AUTOEXEC.BAT file, you can start it by typing XTGOLD (if you have XTreeGold) or XTREE (if you have XTree Easy).

If you didn't request that the installation program change the AUTOEXEC.BAT file, you can make the changes yourself (see the next section). You also can follow these steps to start XTree:

1. Type C: and press Enter to make certain that drive C is the current drive.

2. Type CD \XTGOLD (if you have XTreeGold) or CD \XTREE (if you have XTree Easy) and press Enter.

3. Start XTree by typing XTGOLD (if you have XTreeGold) or XTREE (if you have XTree Easy).

Modifying AUTOEXEC.BAT

AUTOEXEC.BAT is what DOS calls a "batch" file. (A batch file executes the same batch of commands every time you run the file.) AUTOEXEC.BAT is a special batch file, however. If DOS finds this file in the root directory when you start your PC, the commands in AUTOEXEC.BAT execute automatically.

One of the commands you can place in AUTOEXEC.BAT is the PATH command. DOS cannot run a program unless it knows how to find the program. Placing the PATH command in AUTOEXEC.BAT means that DOS can find your program whenever you start the computer.

Another command you can add to AUTOEXEC.BAT is the command to start XTree automatically whenever you start your PC. If you asked the XTree installation program to modify AUTOEXEC.BAT, this command was already added to AUTOEXEC.BAT.

To modify your AUTOEXEC.BAT file, first check to see if an AUTOEXEC.BAT file already exists in the root directory of your hard disk. Enter the following commands:

> C: (to make certain that drive C is the current drive)

> CD \ (to make certain that the root directory is the current directory)

> DIR AUTOEXEC.BAT

If DOS responds by displaying a listing for AUTOEXEC.BAT, the file exists and you can simply modify it. If you see the message File not found, you can create a new AUTOEXEC.BAT file.

To modify an existing AUTOEXEC.BAT file, follow these steps:

1. Type EDLIN AUTOEXEC.BAT and press Enter.

2. When you see the prompt End of input file, press L, and then press Enter.

3. Look for a line that begins with PATH. If you see such a line, notice the number at the beginning of the line. Enter this number and the line redisplays, followed by the line number and a colon. Press F3 to move to the end of the line and type a semicolon (;), but do not press the Enter key. Go to step 5.

4. If no line shows PATH, press L again to see if more lines display. If you find a line starting with PATH, return to step 3. If not, press L again. When all lines have been displayed (the line numbers stop getting larger), and you haven't

found a line starting with PATH, enter a number that is one number larger than the last line number, follow that number with I, and press Enter. Type PATH and press the space bar once. Then go to step 5.

5. Enter the name of your XTree directory and press Enter. If you have installed XTreeGold, the directory name is probably C:\XTGOLD. If you have installed XTree Easy, the directory name is probably C:\XTEASY. The following example shows the results of steps 4 and 5:

```
4: PROMPT $P$G
*5I [press Enter]
5: PATH C:\XTGOLD [press Enter]
```

6. Press E to exit EDLIN and return to DOS. Reboot your system by pressing the Ctrl, Alt, and Del keys at the same time.

7. Start XTree by typing XTGOLD (or XTREE if you are using XTree Easy).

To create a new AUTOEXEC.BAT file, follow these steps:

1. Type COPY CON C:\AUTOEXEC.BAT and press Enter.

2. When the cursor moves down to the next line, type PATH C:\XTGOLD (or PATH C:\XTEASY).

3. Press the space bar, the F6 key, and Enter.

4. Reboot your system by pressing the Ctrl, Alt, and Del keys at the same time.

5. Start XTree by typing XTGOLD (or XTREE if you are using XTree Easy).

In Chapter 4, you will learn how to use XTree's 1Word
text editor to make changes to batch files like
AUTOEXEC.BAT. If you like, you also can modify
AUTOEXEC.BAT so that XTree starts automatically
whenever you start your computer. Simply add
XTGOLD (or XTREE if you are using XTree Easy) as
the last line of AUTOEXEC.BAT.

Reviewing the Screen Display

Figure 3.1 shows the XTree screen with the different
areas of the screen labeled. The current path line
shows the disk and directory path listing for the highlighted directory or file. If you use a mouse, pointing
to the current path line and clicking the left mouse
button activates XTree's drop-down menus.

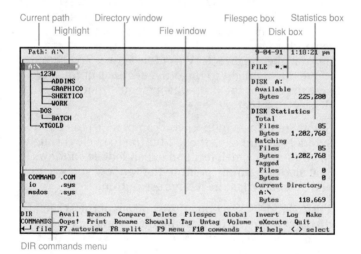

Fig. 3.1. The XTree screen.

The directory window displays a directory tree for the current disk. If the highlight is in the directory window, as shown in figure 3.1, the directory window is the active window. You can move the highlight to other directories on the tree using the arrow keys, PgUp, PgDn, Home, or End. You also can move to another directory by holding down the Shift key and pressing the first letter of the directory name. If two or more directories start with the same letter, XTree highlights each in turn. With the mouse, simply point to the desired directory and click the left mouse button.

The file window contains the list of files in the current directory. When the highlight is in a file window, the file window is active. You move the highlight through the file list using the same keys (or mouse technique) you use to move the highlight in the directory window.

To make a file window active when a directory window is active, press Enter. Press Enter again to display another view of the file window—the expanded file window. Press Enter a third time to again make the directory window active. You cannot move the highlight to the other sections of the XTree screen (except the drop-down menus, which are discussed later).

If you are using a mouse, you can point to the Enter symbol (↵) and click the left button to cycle through the directory, small file, and expanded file windows. You also can simply point to the window you want to activate and click the left mouse button.

The COMMANDS menu at the bottom of the screen displays either directory window commands or file window commands, depending on which type of window is active.

The Filespec box shows the range of files that XTree will display. The default setting in this box, *.*, means that XTree will include all files.

The Disk box shows the current disk drive. This box might not always display the same drive as the current path line, because many of XTree's commands can affect files on more than one drive.

The Statistics box displays information about the files being displayed. Depending on the type of active window, this display changes to show appropriate information.

Selecting a Menu Command

XTree offers several choices when you want to select a command. You can use the keyboard or a mouse to select from menus or, in some cases, you can use "hotkey" shortcut methods to select commands. *Hotkeys* are keystrokes or keystroke combinations (such as Ctrl+T) that select commands directly.

Selecting the Correct Window

Before you select a command, you need to make certain that the highlight is in the correct part of the screen. Refer back to figure 3.1, which shows a typical XTree screen. The highlight is in the upper, or directory, window of the display. Below the directory window is the file window.

XTree has two complete sets of commands, and the set that is active depends on the location of the highlight when you invoke the command or menu.

XTree reminds you of which menu is active by displaying DIR to the left of the menu selections when the directory commands are active. When the file commands are active, FILE replaces DIR. Always make certain that you check which set of commands is active before you make a selection. If the correct

window is not active, press Enter once or twice, as
necessary, to make it active. XTree warns you before
it executes destructive commands, but it does not
verify commands that are not considered destructive.

Selecting a Command

Each command that appears at the bottom of the
screen has a highlighted letter. You can select a command by pressing the highlighted letter or by pointing to the command with the mouse and clicking the
left mouse button. (In this book, the highlighted letter
is shown in bold and blue type.)

Selecting Ctrl and Alt Menu Commands

In addition to having different main menus for the
directory and file windows, XTree has Ctrl and Alt
menus for both windows. These additional menus
have many of the same commands as the main
menus, but the commands are slightly modified when
you also use the Ctrl or Alt key. When you hold down
either the Ctrl or Alt key, the name of the menu
changes by adding CTRL or ALT before FILE or DIR.

Selecting Drop-Down Menu Commands

XTree now also has drop-down menus. These menus
appear whenever you press F10 or click the left
mouse button while the mouse pointer is in the
top line of the screen. The drop-down menus offer a

more organized, easier-to-use method of selecting commands because the commands are separated into groups according to function.

To select a choice on a drop-down menu, highlight your selection using the arrow keys and press Enter. You also can use the mouse by pointing to the selection and clicking the left mouse button.

Getting Help

XTree has an extensive, context-sensitive, on-line help system that covers all of XTree's commands. In addition, technical support is just a phone call or letter away.

Using On-Line Help

To use XTree's help system, follow these steps:

1. Press the F1 key.

   Figure 3.2 shows the main help screen that appears if you press F1 when no command is selected. This help screen shows the different display areas and offers you the opportunity to narrow your search to the specific area that interests you.

2. Highlight the desired topic using the arrow keys, and then press Enter. You also can point at the topic with the mouse pointer and click the left mouse button.

Topics that have additional help screens appear in a different color (or different intensity, if you have a monochrome monitor). The highlight only moves to topics that are available.

```
                          Main Display
This screen shows the various regions of the main XTreeGold display:

        Pull-Down Menus
                                    ┌──────────────────┐
                                    │ FILES:           │
        Directory Window            │                  │
                                    │ DISK:            │
                                    │                  │
                                    │ Statistics       │
        File Window                 │                  │
                                    └──────────────────┘
        Command Menus

        Window Control Keys              Function Keys


Use the ARROW keys to move the highlight bar to the section about which you
want more information and press ENTER.  Select Index to choose from a table
of Help topics or for more information about how to use Help.

┌──────────┐
│Next Page │  Last Page    Back    Dir Commands    File Commands    Index
└──────────┘
←↑↓→ - move cursor              ENTER - select           ESC - exit Help
```

Fig. 3.2. The main XTree help screen.

Using Drop-Down Menu Help

You also can see a description of a command when
you use the drop-down menus. When the drop-down
menus are activated, a description of the highlighted
command appears in the prompt line at the bottom of
the display (see fig. 3.3).

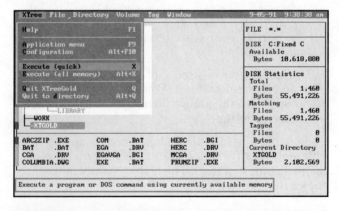

Fig. 3.3. A description of drop-down menu commands appears in the
prompt line.

As figure 3.3 shows, you also can access the on-line Help system through the drop-down menus. Select Help (or press F1) from the XTree drop-down menu to access the Help system immediately.

Obtaining Technical Support

If you have a problem or question with XTree that you cannot resolve, you can call or write the XTree technical support department for assistance. Before you call or write, be sure to locate your serial number. The serial number is listed on the registration card or on your XTree disk. You can also find the serial number within XTree. Hold down the Ctrl and Alt keys at the same time—your serial number appears at the lower right corner of the screen.

For technical support, call

> (805) 541-0604 8 a.m. to 5 p.m. Pacific time, Monday through Friday

or write

> XTree Company
> 4330 Santa Fe Road
> San Luis Obispo, California 93401

In addition, the XTree company has a computer bulletin board system available 24 hours a day. If your computer has a modem, you can dial up this bulletin board and leave questions for the technical support staff, exchange messages with other XTree users, and download free software. To use this system, set your communications program to either 1200 or 2400 bps, 8 data bits, no parity, and 1 stop bit (8N1). Then dial (805) 546-9150.

Changing the Screen Display

XTree has many different screens. The following sections provide a brief description of these screens and show you how to access them.

Viewing the Application Menu

Whether you permit XTree to generate an application menu automatically during installation or you later create your own application menu, XTree can function as a DOS Shell. This capability makes running your programs easy.

You can change to the XTree application menu by pressing F9; you then can later return to the normal XTree display by pressing Esc. Programs are separated into groups based on function.

You can run programs easily from the application menu by highlighting the desired program and pressing Enter or by pointing with the mouse and clicking the left button.

In XTree, the commands attached to each menu item are called a *script*, and each script can contain up to 17 lines of instructions. Scripts are easily modified, so you can change the way any menu item executes. You also can decide whether the applications menu should appear automatically whenever you load XTree. Chapter 7 covers the procedures for creating, using, and modifying application menus in detail.

After examining the application menu, press Esc to return to the XTree main screen.

Understanding the Directory Display

The XTree main screen has two areas that are of primary interest because of their effect on how XTree functions. The first area is the directory window, and the second is the file window.

In XTree, the window containing the highlight is called the *active window*. The active window determines whether directory or file commands are enabled.

To use directory commands, make certain that the highlight is in the directory window by pressing Enter once or twice, as necessary. (Watch for the bottom of the screen menu to display DIR COMMANDS.)

Using a Single-Window Directory Display

Figure 3.4 shows a typical XTree single-window directory display. The highlight is on the A:\ directory—the root directory on the A: drive—and the directory tree for the disk appears in the directory window. Remember that to highlight another directory on the directory tree, you use the arrow keys, PgUp, PgDn, Home, or End. You also can move to another directory by holding down the Shift key and pressing the first letter of the directory name. If two or more directories start with the same letter, XTree highlights each directory in turn. With the mouse, simply point to the directory and click the left mouse button.

The command menu at the bottom of the screen shows DIR COMMANDS, and the statistics box at the right side of the screen shows whole disk information.

```
Path: A:\                                        9-05-91  1:32:27 pm

 A:\                                      FILE  *.*
  ├─123W
  │  ├─ADDINS                             DISK  A:
  │  ├─GRAPHICO                            Available
  │  ├─SHEETICO                             Bytes        225,280
  │  └─WORK
  ├─DOS                                   DISK Statistics
  │  └─BATCH                               Total
  └─XTGOLD                                  Files              85
                                           Bytes       1,202,768
                                          Matching
                                           Files              85
                                           Bytes       1,202,768
                                          Tagged
  COMMAND  .COM                            Files               0
  io       .sys                            Bytes               0
  msdos    .sys                           Current Directory
                                          A:\
                                           Bytes        118,669

DIR          Avail  Branch  Compare  Delete  Filespec  Global   Invert  Log   Make
COMMANDS     Oops!  Print   Rename   Showall  Tag  Untag  Volume  eXecute  Quit
◄─┘ file   F7 autoview   F8 split    F9 menu   F10 commands    F1 help   ‹ › select
```

Fig. 3.4. An XTree single-window directory display.

The commands both at the bottom of the screen menu and in the drop-down menus apply to directories and disks when the highlight is in the directory window. To work with individual files, you must first highlight the file window (see "Understanding the File Display" later in this chapter) by pressing Enter, or by selecting Branch, Showall, or Global.

While the directory window is active, the file window always displays the files that are in the highlighted directory. As you highlight different directories, the file window changes to display the files in the new directory.

 NOTE As long as the filespec that displays in the FILE box in the upper right corner displays *.*, all files in the highlighted directory appear. Chapter 4 explains how to change the filespec to display and use selected groups of files.

The single-window directory display is useful when you are working with a single disk and intend to work with the files in a single directory because it not only shows the directory tree—it includes disk statistics.

Many common directory tasks, such as creating new directories, renaming existing directories, and printing directory information, are also well suited to the single-window directory display.

Using the Split-Window Directory Display

XTree also can show you two directory displays at the same time by splitting the window down the middle. To split the window or return a split window to a single-window display, press F8. You then can move from one side of the display to the other by pressing Tab or pointing with the mouse and clicking the left mouse button. Initially, the split-window display shows two copies of the same directory tree. You can display a different view of the same directory tree, however, by highlighting a different directory on one side of the display or highlighting a view of the directory tree for another disk by using the Log command and selecting the other disk (see fig. 3.5).

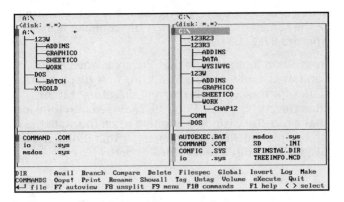

Fig. 3.5. A split-window directory display.

In this case, the left window displays the directory tree for drive A, and the right window displays the directory tree for drive C. Each file window is associated with the directory window above it and displays the files in the highlighted directory in that window.

Split-window directory displays particularly are useful when you want to move directories, copy directory structures, or compare files in different directories. As you will see in upcoming sections, XTree also enables you to have split-window displays with the directory tree in one window and an expanded file display in the other.

Understanding the File Display

Making a file window active enables the file commands. When the file commands are enabled, you can manipulate individual files and groups of files without selecting entire directories. To enable file commands, move the highlight to a file window by pressing Enter (whenever the directory window is active).

When a file window is active, the menu at the bottom of the screen prompts you that the commands available are FILE COMMANDS.

In addition to displaying the File menu when a file window is active, the statistics box now displays statistics for the files in the current directory, rather than the current disk. Don't be confused into thinking that a directory window is active when the statistics box displays DIRECTORY; remember that it displays DISK when a directory window is active.

Using the Small File Window

Depending on the display settings, a small file window can display as few as 4 files at one time, or, on a VGA monitor, as many as 24. Figure 3.6 shows a typical small file window.

```
 Path: A:\DOS                              9-05-91  4:33:17 pm

 A:\                                   FILE  *.*
 ├─123W
 │ ├─ADDINS                            DISK  A:
 │ ├─GRAPHICO                          Available
 │ ├─SHEETICO                            Bytes          225,280
 │ └─WORK
 ├─DOS          ←                      DIRECTORY Stats
 │ └─BATCH                             Total
 └─XTGOLD                                Files               33
                                         Bytes          598,171
                                       Matching
                                         Files               33
                                         Bytes          598,171
                                       Tagged
                                         Files                0
 APPEND   .EXE    CHKDSK .EXE   DISPLAY .SYS    Bytes           0
 ASSIGN   .COM    COMP   .EXE   DOSKEY  .COM  Current File
 ATTRIB   .EXE    DEBUG  .EXE   DRIVER  .SYS    APPEND   .EXE
 BACKUP   .EXE    DISKCOPY.COM  EDLIN   .EXE    Bytes       10,774

FILE       Attributes Copy  Delete  Edit  Filespec  Invert  Log disk  Move
COMMANDS   New date  Open  Print  Rename  Tag  Untag  View  eXecute  Quit
←┘ more   F7 autoview  F8 split   F9 menu  F10 commands    F1 help  ESC cancel
```

Fig. 3.6. An XTree small file window.

Although the small file window is limited in the number of files that it can display, you can easily scroll the window using the arrow keys or the mouse to view files that do not appear. After you select files by highlighting a single file or tagging multiple files, the small file window makes copying or moving files much easier; you can simply point to the destination directory in the directory tree window. (To change from the directory window to a small file window, press Enter or point to the small file window with the mouse and click the left mouse button. If an expanded file window is active, press Enter twice to change to a small file window.)

Using the Expanded File Window

If you press Enter while a small file window is active, XTree expands the file window into the space normally occupied by the directory window, allowing a much larger selection of files to appear (see fig. 3.7).

```
Path: A:\DOS                                    9-05-91  5:04:26 pm
┌────────────────────────────────────┬─────────────────────────┐
│ APPEND   .EXE    LABEL    .EXE      │ FILE  *.*               │
│ ASSIGN   .COM    MEM      .EXE      ├─────────────────────────┤
│ ATTRIB   .EXE    MORE     .COM      │ DISK  A:                │
│ BACKUP   .EXE    MOUSE    .COM      │  Available              │
│ CHKDSK   .EXE    REPLACE  .EXE      │   Bytes        225,280  │
│ COMP     .EXE    RESTORE  .EXE      ├─────────────────────────┤
│ DEBUG    .EXE    SETVER   .EXE      │ DIRECTORY Stats         │
│ DISKCOPY .COM    SHARE    .EXE      │  Total                  │
│ DISPLAY  .SYS    SMARTDRV .SYS      │   Files            33   │
│ DOSKEY   .COM    SORT     .EXE      │   Bytes       598,171   │
│ DRIVER   .SYS    SUBST    .EXE      │  Matching               │
│ EDLIN    .EXE    SYS      .COM      │   Files            33   │
│ EMM386   .EXE    TREE     .COM      │   Bytes       598,171   │
│ FASTOPEN .EXE    XCOPY    .EXE      │  Tagged                 │
│ FC       .EXE                       │   Files             0   │
│ FIND     .EXE                       │   Bytes             0   │
│ FORMAT   .COM                       │  Current File           │
│ HIMEM    .SYS                       │   APPEND    .EXE        │
│ JOIN     .EXE                       │   Bytes        10,774   │
├───────────────────────────────────┴─────────────────────────┤
│ FILE      Attributes  Copy  Delete  Edit  Filespec  Invert  Log disk  Move │
│ COMMANDS  New date  Open  Print  Rename  Tag  Untag  View  eXecute  Quit   │
│ ◄┘ tree   F7 autoview  F8 split   F9 menu  F10 commands  F1 help  ESC cancel│
└──────────────────────────────────────────────────────────────┘
```

Fig. 3.7. The expanded file window.

The expanded file window functions exactly like the
small file window.

Using the Branch File Window

The branch file window is similar to the expanded file
window. In many cases, when you select Branch (on
the directory window menu) to display a branch file
window, you might not see any appreciable difference
from the expanded file window. The reason for this
similarity is simple—the branch file window is a
variation of the expanded file window. The difference
is that the expanded file window displays the files in a
single directory, and the branch file window displays
the files in a directory branch. The branch file window in figure 3.8 demonstrates this difference.

The statistics box now shows BRANCH instead of
DIRECTORY. Also, there are now 34 files instead of 33.
The reason for this change is simple. Figure 3.7 shows
the files in a single directory—A:\DOS. Figure 3.8
shows the files in the same directory, plus any subdirectories. A:\DOS has one subdirectory, BATCH,
that happens to contain the file HOME.BAT.

```
·Path: a:\dos                                    9-05-91  5:14:14 pm

 APPEND    .EXE      JOIN    .EXE        FILE  *.*
 ASSIGN   .COM      LABEL   .EXE
 ATTRIB   .EXE      MEM     .EXE        DISK  A:
 BACKUP   .EXE      MORE    .COM         Available
 CHKDSK   .EXE      MOUSE   .COM          Bytes     225,280
 COMP     .EXE      REPLACE .EXE
 DEBUG    .EXE      RESTORE .EXE        BRANCH Statistics
 DISKCOPY .COM      SETVER  .EXE         Total
 DISPLAY  .SYS      SHARE   .EXE          Files           34
 DOSKEY   .COM      SMARTDRV.SYS          Bytes      598,214
 DRIVER   .SYS      SORT    .EXE         Matching
 EDLIN    .EXE      SUBST   .EXE          Files           34
 EMM386   .EXE      SYS     .COM          Bytes      598,214
 FASTOPEN .EXE      TREE    .COM         Tagged
 FC       .EXE      XCOPY   .EXE          Files            0
 FIND     .EXE                            Bytes            0
 FORMAT   .COM                           Current File
 HIMEM    .SYS                            APPEND   .EXE
 HOME     .BAT                            Bytes       10,774

FILE       Attributes  Copy  Delete  Edit  Filespec  Invert   Log disk  Move
COMMANDS   New date  Open  Print  Rename  Tag  Untag  View   eXecute  Quit
←┘ tree   F7 autoview  F8 split    F9 menu  F10 commands   F1 help   ESC cancel
```

Fig. 3.8. A branch file window.

The branch file window is useful when you want to manipulate files in all subdirectories of a particular directory, as well as those in the highlighted directory. For example, you could use the branch file window to quickly tag all document files in several subdirectories of your word processor program directory.

Using the Showall File Window

The showall file window is another of XTree's variations on the expanded file window. The showall file window displays all files on the current disk. Figure 3.9 shows a showall file window.

To display the showall file window, select Showall from the directory tree menu. The statistics box displays SHOWALL when the showall file window is active. The file window commands remain active when this window appears.

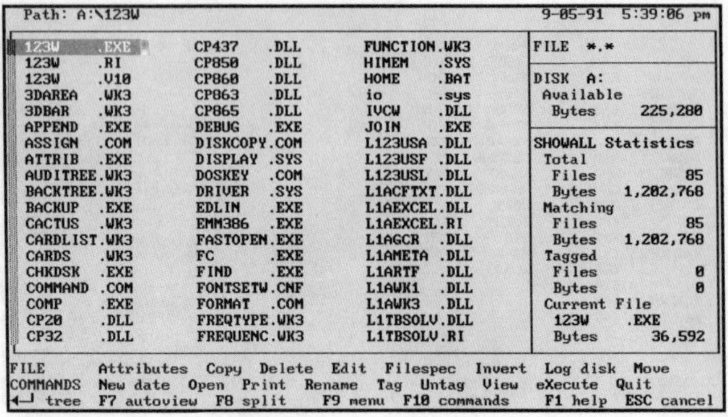

```
Path: A:\123W                                      9-05-91  5:39:06 pm
123W     .EXE    CP437    .DLL    FUNCTION.WK3    FILE  *.*
123W     .RI     CP850    .DLL    HIMEM    .SYS
123W     .V10    CP860    .DLL    HOME     .BAT   DISK A:
3DAREA   .WK3    CP863    .DLL    io       .sys    Available
3DBAR    .WK3    CP865    .DLL    IVCW     .DLL     Bytes      225,280
APPEND   .EXE    DEBUG    .EXE    JOIN     .EXE
ASSIGN   .COM    DISKCOPY.COM     L123USA  .DLL   SHOWALL Statistics
ATTRIB   .EXE    DISPLAY .SYS     L123USF  .DLL    Total
AUDITREE.WK3     DOSKEY  .COM     L123USL  .DLL     Files             85
BACKTREE.WK3     DRIVER  .SYS     L1ACFTXT.DLL      Bytes      1,202,768
BACKUP   .EXE    EDLIN   .EXE     L1AEXCEL.DLL    Matching
CACTUS   .WK3    EMM386  .EXE     L1AEXCEL.RI      Files             85
CARDLIST.WK3     FASTOPEN.EXE     L1AGCR   .DLL     Bytes      1,202,768
CARDS    .WK3    FC      .EXE     L1AMETA  .DLL   Tagged
CHKDSK   .EXE    FIND    .EXE     L1ARTF   .DLL     Files              0
COMMAND  .COM    FONTSETW.CNF     L1AWK1   .DLL     Bytes              0
COMP     .EXE    FORMAT  .COM     L1AWK3   .DLL   Current File
CP20     .DLL    FREQTYPE.WK3     L1TBSOLV.DLL     123W     .EXE
CP32     .DLL    FREQUENC.WK3     L1TBSOLV.RI      Bytes         36,592

FILE         Attributes  Copy Delete  Edit  Filespec   Invert   Move
COMMANDS     New date  Open  Print  Rename  Tag Untag  View  eXecute  Quit
←┘  tree   F7 autoview   F8 split     F9 menu   F10 commands    F1 help  ESC cancel
```

Fig. 3.9. The showall file window.

The showall file window is useful when you want to manipulate files regardless of their location on the disk. The showall file window provides easy access to your entire disk without regard for the directory structure.

Using the Global File Window

The global file window is much like the showall file window. The global file window, however, shows all files on all logged disks. Only the current disk is normally logged when you start XTree. The global file window, therefore, shows exactly the same files as the showall file window, unless you instruct XTree to log additional disks. Before using the directory window G lobal command, use the directory window L og command and specify the disks you want to log. Figure 3.10 shows a global file window.

Global file windows, because they work across both disk and directory structures, can help when you need to compare files on your hard disk to copies on diskettes. You can also use them when you need to find specific files and don't know which directory and disk might contain them.

```
Path: C:\INSET                                         9-06-91  8:48:21 am
$PIX     .TMP    123W     .RI      AA0003  .TDF    FILE  *.*
123      .BAT    123W     .RI      AA012LFA.LRF
123      .DCF    123W     .V10     AA012LHA.LRF    DISK  A:
123      .EXE    123W     .V10     AA024LFA.LRF     Available
123      .HLP    2HIGH    .        AA024LHA.LRF      Bytes      225,280
123      .ICO    3270     .TXT     AC816LFA.LRF
123      .PIF    3DAREA   .FM3     AC816LHA.LRF    GLOBAL Statistics
123      .PIF    3DAREA   .WK3     ACCESS   .COM    Total
123      .VWA    3DAREA   .WK3     ACCESS   .PIF     Files         1,545
123DOS   .EXE    3DBAR    .FM3     ACCTG    .WK3     Bytes    56,693,994
123R2    .ICO    3DBAR    .WK3     ACME_SLS .FM3    Matching
123R23   .BAT    3DBAR    .WK3     ACME_SLS .WK3     Files         1,545
123R23   .ZIP    3DGRAPH  .APP     ADAPTEC  .ZIP     Bytes    56,693,994
123R31   .CNF    3DGRAPH  .HLP     ADDRESS  .DBF    Tagged
123W     .ANN    3DINST   .EXE     ADDRESS  .DTF     Files             0
123W     .EXE    3_BY_7   .INF     ADDRESS  .IDX     Bytes             0
123W     .EXE    0EASE6   .WK3     AF       .BAT    Current File
123W     .HLP    0EASE6   .WK3     AF       .COM     $PIX     .TMP
123W     .INI    AA0003   .BCO     AFH0424  .WR1     Bytes        16,449

FILE        Attributes  Copy  Delete  Edit  Filespec  Invert  Log disk  Move
COMMANDS    New date  Open  Print  Rename  Tag  Untag  View  eXecute  Quit
←┘ tree   F7 autoview   F8 split    F9 menu  F10 commands     F1 help  ESC cancel
```

Fig. 3.10. The global file window.

Splitting the File Window

You can split directory windows using the **F8** key so
that you can display two different directory trees or
two views of the same directory tree. You also can
use **F8** to split file windows, and you can press **Enter**
after splitting the display so that one side is a directory window and the other is a file window. Regardless of the type of split, the active window—the one
containing the highlight—controls which menu is
activated.

Figure 3.11 shows a split screen with an expanded file
window on the left side and a directory window on
the right side. When you split the screen, either side
can contain any of the file window types—small, expanded, branch, showall, or global. Remember, however, that you must use a directory window command
to select the branch, showall, and global file windows.

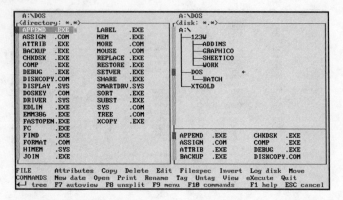

Fig. 3.11. A split window displaying an expanded file window and a directory window.

Summary

In this chapter, you learned how to start XTree and how to understand and use XTree's many different screens. Understanding XTree's screens makes learning the topics presented in the following chapters much easier.

Chapter 4 shows you how to start using XTree for file management.

Managing Files

T his chapter shows you how to use XTree to perform the most common file management functions. Chapters 5 and 6 expand on file management.

Tasks included in the broad area called file management include copying, moving, deleting, renaming,
printing, and editing files. Saving a file is also a file
management task. In fact, you could say that using a
computer without becoming involved in file management is impossible. XTree's file management capabilities are the heart of its power for most users.

Tagging and Untagging Files

The real power of XTree comes from its capability to
work with groups of files that you have tagged. If you
think of tagging files as selecting them, the concept of
tagging becomes clearer.

Unlike DOS, XTree works with groups of files, regardless of whether you can use wild cards to specify the
groups. XTree has a file tag, which is a special marker
that XTree associates with those files you want to
manipulate. After you learn how to tag and untag

files, you can use file tags to help with file management tasks.

Tagged files are marked with a diamond, as you see in figure 4.1. In this figure, ASSIGN.COM, COMP.EXE, and DISKCOPY.COM are all tagged.

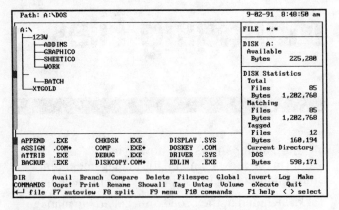

Fig. 4.1. Tagging files in XTree.

XTree enables you to tag and untag individual files whenever a file window is active. That is, the highlight must be in one of the file windows. You cannot tag or untag individual files when the highlight is in a directory window or a view window.

Tagging Individual Files

Tagging individual files gives you the most flexibility. When tagging individual files, you do not have to specify wild cards for file names or file attributes; both procedures can select many more files than you actually want selected. Tagging individual files, however, is the most time-consuming—especially if you must tag a large number of files. At times, you might even find using wild cards to select a group of files faster than tagging the individual files; you would then untag individual files that you did not want included in the group. Tagging files using wild cards and file attributes is covered later in this chapter.

To tag a file—in this case,123W.V10—follow these steps:

1. Highlight the file you want to tag—for this example, highlight 123W.V10.

2. Press T to select Tag. A diamond, which indicates that the file is tagged, appears following the file name (see fig. 4.2).

To use XTree's pull-down menus to tag a file, follow these steps:

1. Highlight the file you want to tag.

2. Press F10 or click the left mouse button in the menu bar to activate the pull-down menus.

3. From the Tag menu, select File.

```
Path: A:\123W                                    9-02-91  2:07:02 pm

123W     .EXE     L1AMETA .DLL        FILE  *.*
123W     .RI      L1ARTF  .DLL
                  L1AWK1  .DLL        DISK  A:
CP20     .DLL     L1AWK3  .DLL          Available
CP32     .DLL     L1TBSOLV.DLL          Bytes      225,280
CP437    .DLL     L1TBSOLV.RI
CP850    .DLL     L1TSOLV .DLL        DIRECTORY Stats
CP860    .DLL     L1TSOLV .RI           Total
CP863    .DLL     L1W3FP  .DLL           Files          33
CP865    .DLL     L1WBASE .FON           Bytes     424,660
FONTSETW.CNF      L1WCAF  .DLL         Matching
IVCW     .DLL     LGICON  .INI           Files          33
L123USA .DLL      LMBSRV  .INI           Bytes     424,660
L123USF .DLL      LOTUS   .BCF         Tagged
L123USL .DLL                             Files           1
L1ACFTXT.DLL                             Bytes           1
L1AEXCEL.DLL                           Current File
L1AEXCEL.RI                              123W    .V10
L1AGCR  .DLL                             Bytes           1

FILE        Attributes  Copy  Delete  Edit  Filespec  Invert   Log disk  Move
COMMANDS    New date  Open  Print  Rename  Tag  Untag  View   eXecute  Quit
←┘ tree  F7 autoview  F8 split    F9 menu  F10 commands    F1 help  ESC cancel
```

Fig. 4.2. An expanded file window with 123W.V10 tagged.

To tag a file using the mouse shortcut method, follow
these steps:

1. Highlight the file you want to tag.

2. Click the right mouse button to tag the file.

NOTE The right mouse button toggles file tags. If
you select a file by highlighting it and then
click the right mouse button, the tag con-
dition for the file is reversed. If the file was
not tagged, it becomes tagged. If the file
already was tagged, it is untagged.

Holding down the Ctrl key when you select Tag tags the entire directory of files.

Untagging Individual Files

To untag a file follow these steps:

1. Highlight the file you want to untag.

2. Select Untag. The diamond disappears, indicat-
ing that the file is now untagged.

To use XTree's pull-down menus to untag a file, follow
these steps:

1. Highlight the file you want to untag.

2. Press F10 or click the left mouse button in the
menu bar to activate the pull-down menus.

3. Select File from the untag section of the Tag
menu.

To untag a file using the mouse shortcut method,
follow these steps:

1. Highlight the file you want to untag.

2. Click the right mouse button to untag the file.

Tagging Multiple Files

Tagging multiple files is more complex than tagging
individual files because you have to determine how to
select the files you want to tag without selecting files
that should not be tagged.

Tagging an Entire Directory

Tagging all the files in a directory is just one step up
from tagging individual files. Figure 4.3 shows a typical XTree display. The A:\DOS directory appears, and
no files are tagged. The directory window is active
(remember to check which menu is displayed by
looking at the lower left part of the screen).

```
 Path: A:\DOS                              9-89-91  7:37:11 am

 A:\                              FILE  *.*
  ├─123W
  │   ├─ADDINS                    DISK  A:
  │   ├─GRAPHICO                  Available
  │   ├─SHEETICO                    Bytes      225,280
  │   └─WORK
  │                              DISK Statistics
  │   └─BATCH                     Total
  └─XTGOLD                          Files            85
                                    Bytes     1,282,768
                                  Matching
                                    Files            85
                                    Bytes     1,282,768
                                  Tagged
                                    Files             0
 APPEND  .EXE   CHKDSK  .EXE   DISPLAY .SYS    Bytes             0
 ASSIGN  .COM   COMP    .EXE   DOSKEY  .COM   Current Directory
 ATTRIB  .EXE   DEBUG   .EXE   DRIVER  .SYS    DOS
 BACKUP  .EXE   DISKCOPY.COM   EDLIN   .EXE    Bytes       598,171

 DIR       Avail  Branch  Compare  Delete  Filespec  Global  Invert  Log  Make
 COMMANDS  Oops!  Print   Rename   Showall  Tag  Untag  Volume  eXecute  Quit
 ◄┘ file   F7 autoview   F8 split     F9 menu   F10 commands   F1 help  < > select
```

Fig. 4.3. The A:\DOS directory with no tagged files.

To use the menu at the bottom of the screen to tag
the files in the A:\DOS directory, follow these steps:

1. Highlight the directory. For the example, make
   sure that the A:\DOS directory is highlighted in
   the directory tree and that the directory window
   is active. If the command menu does not show

DIR COMMANDS, press Enter once or twice, as
needed, to make the directory window active.

2. Press T to select the Tag command. The files in
   the directory are tagged and the highlight
   moves down to the next directory—in this case,
   A:\DOS\BATCH.

3. Press ↑ once to return the highlight to the
   A:\DOS directory. All files in the directory are
   now tagged (see fig. 4.4).

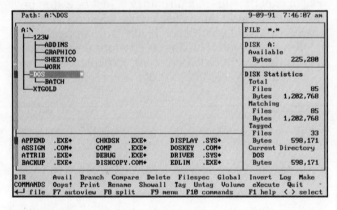

Fig. 4.4. The A:\DOS directory with all files tagged.

If you prefer using XTree's drop-down menus, follow
these steps to tag all files in a directory:

1. Highlight the directory.

2. Press F10 or click the left mouse button while
   the mouse pointer is in the top line of the
   screen.

3. From the Tag menu, press D to select Directory
   files.

   The highlight moves one step down the
   directory tree. Move the highlight back to

the previously highlighted directory (in this case, A:\DOS) either by using ↑ or by pointing with the mouse and clicking the left mouse button.

Mouse users have a quick and easy shortcut method for tagging all files in a directory. Follow these steps:

1. Make sure that the directory you want is high-lighted in the directory tree and the directory window is active. If the command menu does not show DIR COMMANDS or the directory is not highlighted in the directory tree, point to the directory and click the left mouse button.

2. Click the right mouse button to tag the entire directory. Each time you click the right mouse button, you toggle the tagged state of the files.

To multiply the command, press Ctrl +Tag when a directory window is active—the entire disk of files is tagged.

Untagging an Entire Directory

The methods for untagging all files in a directory par-allel the methods for tagging all files in a directory. For example, figure 4.5 shows the drop-down Tag menu for the directory window. The Directory files command in the untag section is highlighted. Select-ing this command untags all files in the currently highlighted directory.

You also can use the directory window Untag com-mand and the file window Ctrl+Untag command to untag all files in a directory. The directory window Ctrl+Untag command untags all files on the disk.

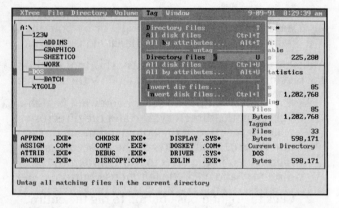

Fig. 4.5. Highlighting the untag Directory files command in the drop-down Tag menu.

Using Wild Cards with Files

XTree uses the filespec in the FILE box to determine which files appear on-screen. (The FILE box is located on the upper right portion of the screen.) Even more important, XTree applies your commands only to those files that match the filespec. You then can limit the effects of a command to a specified group of files within a directory or on a disk.

XTree applies the same wild card conventions as DOS; after you are familiar with wild cards in XTree or DOS, you can understand how they work in the other.

Two wild card characters are available. The asterisk (*) matches any number of characters starting from the current position in either the file name or the extension, and the question mark (?) matches a single character. If the question mark wild card appears at

the end of either the file name or the extension specification, it matches either a single character or no
characters.

Figure 4.6 shows the files in the A:\DOS directory in
an expanded file window. The filespec (shown in the
FILE box) is XTree's default of *.*.

```
 Path: A:\DOS                                      9-09-91  9:32:32 am
┌──────────────────────────────────────────────┐┌─────────────────────┐
│APPEND  .EXE      LABEL   .EXE                  ││FILE  *.*            │
│ASSIGN  .COM      MEM     .EXE                  ││                     │
│ATTRIB  .EXE      MORE    .COM                  ││DISK  A:             │
│BACKUP  .EXE      MOUSE   .COM                  ││ Available           │
│CHKDSK  .EXE      REPLACE .EXE                  ││   Bytes      225,280│
│COMP    .EXE      RESTORE .EXE                  ││                     │
│DEBUG   .EXE      SETVER  .EXE                  ││DIRECTORY Stats      │
│DISKCOPY.COM      SHARE   .EXE                  ││ Total               │
│DISPLAY .SYS      SMARTDRV.SYS                  ││  Files           33 │
│DOSKEY  .COM      SORT    .EXE                  ││  Bytes      598,171 │
│DRIVER  .SYS      SUBST   .EXE                  ││ Matching            │
│EDLIN   .EXE      SYS     .COM                  ││  Files           33 │
│EMM386  .EXE      TREE    .COM                  ││  Bytes      598,171 │
│FASTOPEN.EXE      XCOPY   .EXE                  ││ Tagged              │
│FC      .EXE                                    ││  Files            0 │
│FIND    .EXE                                    ││  Bytes            0 │
│FORMAT  .COM                                    ││ Current File        │
│HIMEM   .SYS                                    ││  APPEND  .EXE       │
│JOIN    .EXE                                    ││  Bytes       10,774 │
└──────────────────────────────────────────────┘└─────────────────────┘
FILE        Attributes  Copy  Delete  Edit  Filespec  Invert  Log disk  Move
COMMANDS    New date  Open  Print  Rename  Tag  Untag  View  eXecute  Quit
←┘ tree    F7 autoview    F8 split    F9 menu  F10 commands    F1 help  ESC cancel
```

Fig. 4.6. XTree's default filespec is *.*.

To change the filespec and limit the range of displayed files, follow these steps:

1. Select **F**ilespec by pressing **F**. If you press ↑,
   XTree displays a command history—the last
   16 responses you gave when using the **F**ilespec
   command. Figure 4.7 shows a typical command
   history.

2. If you want to reuse one of your past responses,
   use ↑ or the mouse pointer to highlight the response; then press **Enter**.

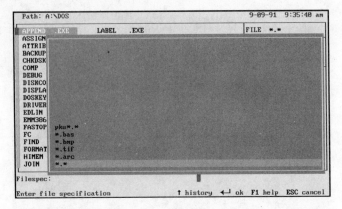

Fig. 4.7. An XTree command history for the Filespec command.

To enter a new filespec, press Esc. Enter or edit the
file name or wild card specification at the Filespec:
prompt and press Enter. Figure 4.8 shows the effect
of changing the filespec to *.COM.

```
Path: A:\DOS                          9-09-91  9:36:28 am
ASSIGN   .COM              FILE  *.COM
DISKCOPY.COM
DOSKEY   .COM              DISK  A:
FORMAT   .COM              Available
MORE     .COM                Bytes      225,280
MOUSE    .COM
SYS      .COM              DIRECTORY Stats
TREE     .COM              Total
                            Files          33
                            Bytes      598,171
                           Matching
                            Files           8
                            Bytes      111,778
                           Tagged
                            Files           0
                            Bytes           0
                           Current File
                            ASSIGN   .COM
                            Bytes        6,399

FILE      Attributes  Copy  Delete  Edit  Filespec  Invert  Log disk  Move
COMMANDS  New date  Open  Print  Rename  Tag  Untag  View  eXecute  Quit
←┘ tree   F7 autoview  F8 split    F9 menu  F10 commands    F1 help  ESC cancel
```

Fig. 4.8. The effect of using *.COM as the filespec.

To understand the way that XTree uses wild cards,
use the Ctrl+Tag command to tag all the files that
appear in the current directory.

Next, use the Filespec command again and return the
filespec to the default of *.* to display all files. When
you change the filespec, XTree does not change the
tagged state of files. As you see in figure 4.9, only files
with a COM extension are tagged. By using wild
cards, you can tag some files in the directory without
affecting any other files. You then can use additional
wild cards to tag more file groups or tag (or untag)
individual files. Because most XTree commands oper-
ate only on tagged files, you easily can select exactly
the files you want by tagging—using both wild cards
and individual selection. Later, you will learn how to
use file attributes to control further which files are
tagged.

```
 Path: A:\DOS                                    9-09-91 11:01:04 am
┌────────────────────────────────────────────┬─────────────────────┐
│ APPEND   .EXE      LABEL   .EXE             │ FILE  *.*           │
│ ASSIGN  .COM♦      MEM     .EXE             │                     │
│ ATTRIB  .EXE       MORE    .COM♦            │ DISK  A:            │
│ BACKUP  .EXE       MOUSE   .COM♦            │ Available           │
│ CHKDSK  .EXE       REPLACE .EXE             │  Bytes      225,280 │
│ COMP    .EXE       RESTORE .EXE             │                     │
│ DEBUG   .EXE       SETVER  .EXE             │ DIRECTORY Stats     │
│ DISKCOPY.COM♦      SHARE   .EXE             │ Total               │
│ DISPLAY .SYS       SMARTDRV.SYS             │  Files           33 │
│ DOSKEY  .COM♦      SORT    .EXE             │  Bytes      598,171 │
│ DRIVER  .SYS       SUBST   .EXE             │ Matching            │
│ EDLIN   .EXE       SYS     .COM♦            │  Files           33 │
│ EMM386  .EXE       TREE    .COM♦            │  Bytes      598,171 │
│ FASTOPEN.EXE       XCOPY   .EXE             │ Tagged              │
│ FC      .EXE                                │  Files            8 │
│ FIND    .EXE                                │  Bytes      111,778 │
│ FORMAT  .COM♦                               │ Current File        │
│ HIMEM   .SYS                                │  APPEND   .EXE      │
│ JOIN    .EXE                                │  Bytes       10,774 │
├────────────────────────────────────────────┴─────────────────────┤
│ FILE      Attributes  Copy  Delete  Edit  Filespec  Invert  Log disk  Move │
│ COMMANDS  New date  Open  Print  Rename  Tag  Untag  View  eXecute  Quit │
│ ←┘ tree   F7 autoview  F8 split    F9 menu  F10 commands    F1 help  ESC cancel │
└───────────────────────────────────────────────────────────────────┘
```

Fig. 4.9. Only files with a COM extension are tagged.

You might have noticed the Filespec command on
both the directory window menu and the file window
menu. The same command also appears on the
Window drop-down menu in both directory and file
windows. The location of this command is not important; in fact, selecting it from any of the four menus
has exactly the same effect.

Viewing and Changing File Attributes

DOS uses a special section of each file's directory entry to record certain information—the file attributes. You can use file attribute information to protect your files and to assist in simplifying common file management tasks, such as backing up files. You also can use file attributes to help control which files XTree tags for further processing.

DOS uses six file attributes. A file might be marked as a read-only, hidden, system, volume label, subdirectory, or archive entry. The volume label and subdirectory attributes are normally not applied to files and cannot be set using XTree. Of the remaining four, the read-only, hidden, and system attributes prevent files from being overwritten or deleted. Normally, the read-only attribute is the best choice of these three, because the other two also hide the file. The archive attribute signals when a file has been changed. XTree can use any of the four attributes to control which files are tagged.

 **NOTE** Do not confuse the archive file attribute with the process of archiving files. The archive file attribute simply marks that a file has been modified since the last backup. Archiving files refers to compressing them and storing them in library files (called *archives*) that take up considerably less disk space.

Viewing File Attributes

XTree offers three different views of file listings. The first, which is the default setting, displays only the file name and extension. (Refer to fig. 4.9, which shows the expanded file window using the default view of file listings.)

The other two views of the file listings show more information about each file at the expense of fewer files displayed in each list. The default view has room for three columns of files. The second view, which adds both file attribute and file size information, has room for only two columns. The third view, which shows file attributes, file size, and creation or modification date and time, has room to display only a single column of files. Figure 4.10 shows the two-column and figure 4.11 shows the one-column file listing.

Press Alt+File Display to change the number of displayed columns. You can use this command in either the directory window or a file window.

```
 Path: A:\DOS                                     9-09-91 12:37:04 pm
┌──────────────────────────┬─────────────────────────┬───────────────────────┐
│ APPEND   .EXE  10,774 ....│ LABEL    .EXE   9,390 ....│ FILE  *.*            │
│ ASSIGN   .COM   6,399 ....│ MEM      .EXE  39,818 ....│                     │
│ ATTRIB   .EXE  15,796 ....│ MORE     .COM   2,618 .a..│ DISK  A:            │
│ BACKUP   .EXE  36,092 ....│ MOUSE    .COM  31,833 ....│ Available           │
│ CHKDSK   .EXE  16,200 ....│ REPLACE  .EXE  20,226 .a..│   Bytes    225,280 │
│ COMP     .EXE  14,282 ....│ RESTORE  .EXE  38,294 ....│                     │
│ DEBUG    .EXE  20,634 ....│ SETVER   .EXE  12,007 .a..│ DIRECTORY Stats     │
│ DISKCOPY .COM  11,793 ....│ SHARE    .EXE  10,912 ....│ Total               │
│ DISPLAY  .SYS  15,792 ....│ SMARTDRV .SYS   8,335 ....│   Files         33 │
│ DOSKEY   .COM   5,883 .a..│ SORT     .EXE   6,938 ....│   Bytes    598,171 │
│ DRIVER   .SYS   5,409 ....│ SUBST    .EXE  18,478 ....│ Matching            │
│ EDLIN    .EXE  12,642 ....│ SYS      .COM  13,440 ....│   Files         33 │
│ EMM386   .EXE  91,742 ....│ TREE     .COM   6,901 ....│   Bytes    598,171 │
│ FASTOPEN .EXE  12,050 ....│ XCOPY    .EXE  15,804 .a..│ Tagged              │
│ FC       .EXE  18,650 ....│                          │   Files          0 │
│ FIND     .EXE   6,770 ....│                          │   Bytes          0 │
│ FORMAT   .COM  32,911 ....│                          │ Current File        │
│ HIMEM    .SYS  11,488 ....│                          │   APPEND    .EXE    │
│ JOIN     .EXE  17,870 ....│                          │   Bytes     10,774 │
├──────────────────────────┴─────────────────────────┴───────────────────────┤
│ FILE        Attributes  Copy  Delete  Edit  Filespec  Invert  Log disk  Move│
│ COMMANDS    New date  Open  Print  Rename  Tag  Untag  View  eXecute  Quit  │
│ ↵ tree   F7 autoview   F8 split     F9 menu   F10 commands    F1 help  ESC cancel│
└─────────────────────────────────────────────────────────────────────────────┘
```

Fig. 4.10. The two-column file listing.

```
 Path: A:\DOS                                    9-09-91 12:37:30 pm
┌────────────────────────────────────────────┬───────────────────────┐
│ APPEND   .EXE   10,774 ....  4-09-91  5:00:00 am │ FILE  *.*             │
│ ASSIGN   .COM    6,399 ....  4-09-91  5:00:00 am │                       │
│ ATTRIB   .EXE   15,796 ....  4-09-91  5:00:00 am │ DISK  A:              │
│ BACKUP   .EXE   36,092 ....  4-09-91  5:00:00 am │  Available            │
│ CHKDSK   .EXE   16,200 ....  4-09-91  5:00:00 am │   Bytes       225,280 │
│ COMP     .EXE   14,282 ....  4-09-91  5:00:00 am │                       │
│ DEBUG    .EXE   20,634 ....  4-09-91  5:00:00 am │ DIRECTORY Stats       │
│ DISKCOPY.COM    11,793 ....  4-09-91  5:00:00 am │  Total                │
│ DISPLAY  .SYS   15,792 ....  4-09-91  5:00:00 am │   Files            33 │
│ DOSKEY   .COM    5,883 .a..  4-09-91  5:00:00 am │   Bytes       598,171 │
│ DRIVER   .SYS    5,409 ....  4-09-91  5:00:00 am │  Matching             │
│ EDLIN    .EXE   12,642 ....  4-09-91  5:00:00 am │   Files            33 │
│ EMM386   .EXE   91,742 ....  4-09-91  5:00:00 am │   Bytes       598,171 │
│ FASTOPEN.EXE    12,050 ....  4-09-91  5:00:00 am │  Tagged               │
│ FC       .EXE   18,650 ....  4-09-91  5:00:00 am │   Files             0 │
│ FIND     .EXE    6,770 ....  4-09-91  5:00:00 am │   Bytes             0 │
│ FORMAT   .COM   32,911 ....  4-09-91  5:00:00 am │  Current File         │
│ HIMEM    .SYS   11,488 ....  3-08-91  5:05:00 am │   APPEND   .EXE       │
│ JOIN     .EXE   17,870 ....  4-09-91  5:00:00 am │   Bytes        10,774 │
├────────────────────────────────────────────┴───────────────────────┤
│ FILE      Attributes  Copy  Delete  Edit  Filespec  Invert  Log disk  Move │
│ COMMANDS  New date  Open  Print  Rename  Tag  Untag  View  eXecute  Quit │
│ ←┘ tree   F7 autoview  F8 split    F9 menu  F10 commands   F1 help  ESC cancel │
└─────────────────────────────────────────────────────────────────────┘
```

Fig. 4.11. The one-column file listing.

These figures include several files that have their
archive file attribute set, which is indicated by .a..
following the file name and extension. The other
three file attributes that XTree can modify also might
be set; r indicates read-only, s indicates system, and
h indicates hidden.

NOTE DOS uses the hidden and system file
attributes together for two necessary
DOS files. IO.SYS and MSDOS.SYS (or
IBMDOS.COM and IBMBIO.COM) must be
in the root directory of the disk used to
boot your PC. These two files are automatically given both the hidden and system file attributes. Do not change the file
attributes for these two files or you might
prevent your system from operating.

Using File Attributes

Earlier, you learned that XTree can use file attributes
to control which files are tagged. Because XTree

applies commands to tagged files, being able to tag files based on their file attributes increases the available options.

Refer to figure 4.10, which shows five files that have their archive file attribute set. These five files have probably been modified since the last backup, although the archive file attribute also can be set using XTree or DOS. If the modified files are data files, you can use the archive attribute to determine which data files have been updated and, therefore, need to be backed up.

XTree goes a step further. Using file attributes to control which files are tagged means you can execute any XTree function based on file attributes. To tag files using file attributes, follow these steps:

1. Highlight the correct directory and make certain that a file window is active.

2. If you want to check the attributes already assigned to files, hold down the Alt key and press F once for a two-column display or twice for a one-column display.

3. Hold down the Alt key and press T to select the Tag command. XTree then prompts you to enter the list of attributes to use in selecting the files to tag. You can enter any combination of the four attributes. Precede each attribute with a plus (+) to indicate that the attribute must be set or a minus (–) to indicate that the attribute must not be set. XTree ignores any file attributes that are not included in your list.

   Figure 4.12 shows +A, which means that only the archive attribute will be checked to determine which files should be tagged.

4. Press Enter to execute the command. Figure 4.13 shows the result of pressing Enter.

```
Path: A:\DOS                                          9-09-91  3:01:01 pm
┌────────────────────────────────────────────────┬──────────────────────┐
│ APPEND  .EXE   10,774 ....   LABEL   .EXE  9,390 ....│ FILE  *.*         │
│ ASSIGN  .COM    6,399 ....   MEM     .EXE 39,818 ....│                   │
│ ATTRIB  .EXE   15,796 ....   MORE    .COM  2,618 .a..│ DISK A:           │
│ BACKUP  .EXE   36,092 ....   MOUSE   .COM 31,833 ....│ Available         │
│ CHKDSK  .EXE   16,200 ....   REPLACE .EXE 20,226 .a..│   Bytes    225,280│
│ COMP    .EXE   14,282 ....   RESTORE .EXE 38,294 ....│                   │
│ DEBUG   .EXE   20,634 ....   SETVER  .EXE 12,007 .a..│ DIRECTORY Stats   │
│ DISKCOPY.COM   11,793 ....   SHARE   .EXE 10,912 ....│ Total             │
│ DISPLAY .SYS   15,792 ....   SMARTDRV.SYS  8,335 ....│   Files        33 │
│ DOSKEY  .COM    5,883 .a..   SORT    .EXE  6,938 ....│   Bytes   598,171 │
│ DRIVER  .SYS    5,409 ....   SUBST   .EXE 18,478 ....│ Matching          │
│ EDLIN   .EXE   12,642 ....   SYS     .COM 13,440 ....│   Files        33 │
│ EMM386  .EXE   91,742 ....   TREE    .COM  6,901 ....│   Bytes   598,171 │
│ FASTOPEN.EXE   12,050 ....   XCOPY   .EXE 15,804 .a..│ Tagged            │
│ FC      .EXE   18,650 ....                           │   Files         0 │
│ FIND    .EXE    6,770 ....                           │   Bytes         0 │
│ FORMAT  .COM   32,911 ....                           │ Current File      │
│ HIMEM   .SYS   11,488 ....                           │   APPEND   .EXE   │
│ JOIN    .EXE   17,870 ....                           │   Bytes    10,774 │
├────────────────────────────────────────────────┴──────────────────────┤
│TAG ALL MATCHING FILES BY ATTRIBUTES                                     │
│             │  :  +A  │                                                  │
│Enter attributes (+/- RASH)          ↑ history  ◄─┘ ok  F1 help ESC cancel│
└─────────────────────────────────────────────────────────────────────────┘
```

Fig. 4.12. Specifying the archive attribute as the selector for tagging files.

```
Path: A:\DOS                                          9-09-91  3:01:22 pm
┌────────────────────────────────────────────────┬──────────────────────┐
│ APPEND  .EXE   10,774 ....   LABEL   .EXE   9,390 ....│ FILE  *.*        │
│ ASSIGN  .COM    6,399 ....   MEM     .EXE  39,818 ....│                  │
│ ATTRIB  .EXE   15,796 ....   MORE    .COM♦  2,618 .a..│ DISK A:          │
│ BACKUP  .EXE   36,092 ....   MOUSE   .COM  31,833 ....│ Available        │
│ CHKDSK  .EXE   16,200 ....   REPLACE .EXE♦ 20,226 .a..│   Bytes   225,280│
│ COMP    .EXE   14,282 ....   RESTORE .EXE  38,294 ....│                  │
│ DEBUG   .EXE   20,634 ....   SETVER  .EXE♦ 12,007 .a..│ DIRECTORY Stats  │
│ DISKCOPY.COM   11,793 ....   SHARE   .EXE  10,912 ....│ Total            │
│ DISPLAY .SYS   15,792 ....   SMARTDRV.SYS   8,335 ....│   Files       33 │
│ DOSKEY  .COM♦   5,883 .a..   SORT    .EXE   6,938 ....│   Bytes  598,171 │
│ DRIVER  .SYS    5,409 ....   SUBST   .EXE  18,478 ....│ Matching         │
│ EDLIN   .EXE   12,642 ....   SYS     .COM  13,440 ....│   Files       33 │
│ EMM386  .EXE   91,742 ....   TREE    .COM   6,901 ....│   Bytes  598,171 │
│ FASTOPEN.EXE   12,050 ....   XCOPY   .EXE♦ 15,804 .a..│ Tagged           │
│ FC      .EXE   18,650 ....                            │   Files        5 │
│ FIND    .EXE    6,770 ....                            │   Bytes   56,538 │
│ FORMAT  .COM   32,911 ....                            │ Current File     │
│ HIMEM   .SYS   11,488 ....                            │   APPEND   .EXE  │
│ JOIN    .EXE   17,870 ....                            │   Bytes   10,774 │
├────────────────────────────────────────────────┴──────────────────────┤
│FILE      Attributes  Copy  Delete  Edit  Filespec  Invert  Log disk  Move│
│COMMANDS  New date  Open  Print  Rename  Tag  Untag  View  eXecute  Quit  │
│◄─┘ tree  F7 autoview  F8 split    F9 menu  F10 commands   F1 help ESC cancel│
└─────────────────────────────────────────────────────────────────────────┘
```

Fig. 4.13. The result of tagging by attribute.

> **CAUTION:** Always make certain that the correct window is active before you execute XTree commands.

The drop-down menus also enable you to tag files based on file attributes. To use the drop-down menus, follow these steps:

1. Highlight the correct directory and make certain that a file window is active (or a directory window, if you want to tag all files on the disk by file attributes).

2. From the Tag drop-down menu, press B to select the All by attributes command.

3. Enter any combination of the four attributes to select files to tag. Precede each attribute with a plus sign (+) to indicate that the attribute must be set or a minus sign (–) to indicate that the attribute must not be set. XTree ignores file attributes that are not included in your list.

As with the Tag command, Alt+Tag has an equivalent untagging command, Alt+Untag. You can use Alt+Untag to untag files based on any combination of the four file attributes that XTree uses.

Changing File Attributes

You can only change file attributes when a file window is active. You can, however, decide whether to change the attributes of a single file or a series of tagged files. Remember that XTree's optional file windows—branch, showall, and global—expand the range of displayed files. You easily can change file attributes for the range from a single file to all files on your disk.

To change file attributes for a single file at a time, follow these steps:

1. Make certain that a file window is active.

2. Highlight the file whose attributes you want to change.

3. From the File Commands menu, press A to select Attributes.

4. Enter the new set of attributes. Use a plus sign (+) directly in front of an attribute to set the

attribute; use a minus sign (–) to turn it off. Do not include any spaces between attributes.

5. Press **Enter** to make the changes.

To change file attributes on multiple files, follow these steps:

1. Tag the files you want to change. The method you use to tag the files depends on the group of files you want to change.

2. Make certain a file window is active.

3. Press **Ctrl+Attributes**.

4. Enter the new set of attributes. Use a plus sign (+) directly in front of an attribute to set the attribute; use a minus sign (–) to turn it off. Do not include any spaces between attributes.

5. Press **Enter** to make the changes.

CAUTION: XTree uses file tags when modifying file attributes on multiple files. Be sure that you have the correct group of files tagged before you issue the command to change the attributes. If you make a mistake and change file attributes for the wrong group of files, correcting the mistake might be difficult. Correcting mistakes can be especially difficult if you modify the hidden, system, or read-only file attributes because you might not know what each file's attributes should be.

Changing File Attributes before Backups

Understanding file attributes and knowing how to view and change them can help make many common tasks much easier. Few PC users, for example, are nearly as conscientious as they should be about backing up files. Most users put off the task. Intelligent use of both the BACKUP command's options and XTree's capability to change file attributes can greatly reduce both the time involved and the number of disks required to do a backup.

Consider the main reason for doing backups—to protect your data from accidental erasure or a hard disk failure. Remember, you can usually reinstall your programs using the original disks, but your data is the result of hours of hard work. Often, replacing data files would be difficult if not impossible. When planning backups, make certain that you back up what really needs to be backed up without wasting time making more copies of program files.

The following rules can help you to make backing up your data much faster and easier:

- Always place your data files in separate subdirectories under your program directories.

- Use XTree to turn the archive file attribute off for all files in your program directories immediately after installing a program.

- Use the /M switch with the BACKUP command to back up only those files whose archive file attribute is turned on.

- Use the /S switch with the BACKUP command to back up files in subdirectories.

- Use the /A switch with the BACKUP command to add backup files to a disk already containing backed up files.

The BACKUP command turns the archive file attribute off when it backs up a file. Therefore, if you use the /M switch, XTree will not back up files that weren't modified between backups. Backing up files after the first backup is then faster because fewer files need to be backed up.

Copying Files

Copying files to other directories or disks is one of the most common file management functions that nearly every PC user encounters. Moving files from one place to another is another closely related task, but because DOS doesn't have a move command, most people think in terms of two operations—first a copy and then a delete. (See the section "Moving Files" later in this chapter.) XTree makes copying and moving files simple operations.

Copying a Single File

XTree can quickly copy a single file to another directory or another disk. Copying a single file does not require the file to be tagged, so you can copy a file that is not tagged whether or not other files are tagged.

Before you can copy files, one of the file windows must be the active window. You might find that copying is more convenient if you use a split window display. One side of the screen then can be an expanded file window, and the other side can display a directory window. This setup enables you easily to select the file to copy in the expanded file window. You then can point to the target directory in the directory window. Figure 4.14 shows an example of this type of split window display.

```
A:\DOS\BATCH                    C:\DOS\BATCH
┌<disk: *.*>─────────          ┌<directory: *.*>──────
 A:\                             123     .BAT      44 .a..
   └──123W                       123R23  .BAT      23 .a..
      ├──ADDINS                  2HIGH   .          3 ....
      ├──GRAPHICO                AF      .BAT      14 ....
      ├──SHEETICO                AFS     .BAT      31 ....
      └──WORK                    CAD     .BAT      33 ....
   ┌──DOS                        CSAN    .BAT      37 ....
   │  └──BATCH        ←          FORMFEED.BAT       2 ....
   └──XTGOLD                     IN      .BAT      41 .a..
                                 INC     .BAT      20 ....
                                 LET     .BAT      56 ....
                                 LISTARC .BAT     115 ....
                                 LISTARC1.BAT      43 ....
                                 LISTZIP .BAT     127 .a..
                                 LISTZIP1.BAT      48 ....
 HOME     .BAT    43 .a..        NEW-VARS.BAT     180 ....
                                 QA      .BAT      30 ....
                                 QC      .BAT     336 ....
                                 SHOWARC .BAT      48 ....

FILE         Attributes  Copy  Delete  Edit  Filespec  Invert   Log disk  Move
COMMANDS     New date  Open  Print  Rename  Tag  Untag  View  eXecute  Quit
◄┘ tree   F7 autoview   F8 unsplit   F9 menu   F10 commands   F1 help   ESC cancel
```

Fig. 4.14. A split window display makes file copying easier.

Suppose that you wanted to copy the batch file 123.BAT from the C:\DOS\BATCH directory to the A:\DOS\BATCH directory. Follow these steps:

1. Use the F8 key to split the window display.

2. If the destination drive has not been logged (or read) by XTree, select the Log disk command and specify the disk to log. In this case, enter A as the disk to log.

3. Display a directory tree window on the side of the screen that is logged onto the destination drive. This display will be the default, so you should not have to change the window. Highlight the destination directory. In this case, highlight A:\DOS\BATCH.

4. On the other side of the split window display, highlight the source directory in the directory window (use the Tab key or point with the mouse to change sides of the split). Press Enter twice to change to an expanded file window. In this example, highlight C:\DOS\BATCH.

5. Highlight the file you want to copy. Use the arrow keys or the mouse to highlight the file. In this example, highlight 123.BAT.

6. Select Copy. If you want to keep the same name for the file, press Enter at the prompt. In this case, the prompt shows

    ```
    COPY file: 123.BAT as
    ```

    If you want to rename the file while copying it, enter the new name before pressing Enter.

    The to: prompt shows the destination directory.

7. If the correct destination directory does not appear, type a new destination directory. You can also press F2 or click the mouse to highlight a different destination directory.

8. Press Enter to begin the copy. Select Yes to have XTree automatically replace an existing file in the destination directory or No to have XTree prompt you before copying over a file with the same name. XTree copies the file, but it does not automatically update the list of files displayed in the destination directory until you again select that directory. Figure 4.15 shows that file was indeed copied.

You can also use the drop-down menus to copy the file. In step 6, select Copy from the File drop-down menu. Otherwise, every other step remains the same.

```
A:\DOS\BATCH                    C:\DOS\BATCH
<disk: *.*>─────────────       <directory: *.*>─────────────
A:\                            │123    .BAT     44 .a..
 └─123W                         123R23 .BAT     23 .a..
   ├─ADDINS                     2HIGH  .         3 ....
   ├─GRAPHICO                   AF     .BAT     14 ....
   ├─SHEETICO                   AFS    .BAT .   31 ....
   └─WORK                       CAD    .BAT     33 ....
 ├─DOS                          CSAN   .BAT     37 ....
 │ └─BATCH           ▌          FORMFEED.BAT     2 ....
 └─XTGOLD                       IN     .BAT     41 .a..
                                INC    .BAT     20 ....
                                LET    .BAT     56 ....
                                LISTARC .BAT   115 ....
                                LISTARC1.BAT    43 ....
                                LISTZIP .BAT   127 .a..
                                LISTZIP1.BAT    48 ....
 123    .BAT     44 .a..        NEW-VARS.BAT   180 ....
 HOME   .BAT     43 .a..        QA     .BAT     30 ....
                                QC     .BAT    336 ....
                                SHOWARC .BAT    48 ....

DIR       Avail  Branch  Compare  Delete  Filespec  Global   Invert  Log  Make
COMMANDS  Oops!  Print   Rename   Showall  Tag  Untag  Volume  eXecute  Quit
←┘ file   F7 autoview  F8 unsplit  F9 menu  F10 commands   F1 help  < > select
```

Fig. 4.15. 123.BAT was copied to A:\DOS\BATCH.***

Copying Multiple Files

Before you can copy multiple files with a single command, tag the files you want to copy. You can use any of the methods discussed earlier to tag the files. The files you want to copy will determine the method (or combination of methods) you select.

To copy tagged files, first complete steps 1 through 4 in the section "Copying a Single File," if you have not already done so. Then follow these steps:

1. Tag the files by highlighting each in turn and selecting Tag or by pointing to the files with the mouse and clicking the right mouse button.

2. Select Copy files from the Tagged drop-down menu .

   If you prefer, you can press Ctrl+Copy instead of using the drop-down menus.

3. Press Enter in response to the COPY all tagged files as prompt. XTree is asking if you want to change the file names while copying. Although you could specify a wild card expression for renaming the files, specifying a single file name would result in all four files being copied to the same file. The resulting file would only contain the data from the last file copied.

4. Press Enter if the correct destination directory appears on-screen. You also can type a new destination directory and press Enter in response to the to: prompt.

5. Select Yes to have XTree replace existing files in the destination directory automatically or No to have XTree prompt you before copying over a file with the same name. As XTree copies the tagged files, it moves the highlight to show which file is being copied. Because XTree does not automatically update the destination directory display, you must highlight the destination directory in the directory window to confirm that the directory contains the files.

XTree will not copy files if the operation would replace an existing file that has either a system or a hidden file attribute. If you must replace files with either of these file attributes, first change the file attributes of the existing file to remove these attributes. Use extreme care, however, when replacing files that have these attributes—DOS uses the hidden and system file attributes to protect some of its vital files.

XTree prompts you before it copies over a file that has a read-only file attribute, even if you specified for XTree to replace existing files in the destination directory automatically. Again, use care when replacing files that have the read-only file attribute.

In addition to copying single files or tagged files, XTree also can copy files along with the directory structure that contains them. Chapter 6 covers this subject.

Moving Files

DOS does not offer a single command that compares to the XTree Move command. Moving files using DOS commands requires that you first type a command to copy the files and then type another command to delete the source files. XTree performs this function in a single step. Also, because XTree can move groups of tagged files, a single XTree move can replace several copy and delete steps.

Moving files with XTree also is safer than moving files using DOS copy and delete commands. Using the DOS commands, you have the potential for disk errors on the destination disk. If you didn't notice these errors, they could result in a bad or nonexistent copy, which could be disastrous if you deleted your only good original.

Another possible error results from having to type two DOS commands, both requiring a file name. If you accidently type a different name as the argument for the delete command than the copy command, you could delete a file that you didn't copy.

XTree treats moving files as a simple extension of copying files. You can move a single file or multiple files that you have tagged. In Chapter 6, you will learn how to move files along with their directory structure.

 NOTE You cannot move files that have read-only, hidden, or system file attributes. XTree requires that you remove these attributes before you can move the files.

Moving a Single File

To see how XTree handles moving files, suppose that you discovered that several batch files had accidentally been copied to the A:\DOS directory instead of to the A:\DOS\BATCH directory, and you want to move the files to the correct directory.

To move a single file, follow these steps:

1. Create a split screen display with the destination directory highlighted in the directory window on one side of the split. In this case, A:\DOS\BATCH is the destination directory.

2. Switch to the other side of the split and highlight the source directory. Press Enter twice to change the window to an expanded file window. A:\DOS is the source directory in this example.

3. Highlight the file that you want to move—in this case, NEW-VARS.BAT.

4. Select Move from either the drop-down File menu or from the FILE COMMANDS menu at the bottom of the screen.

5. At the prompt, press Enter or type a new file name.

6. At the to: prompt, press Enter or type a new destination directory if the correct directory does not appear (see fig. 4.16). Select Yes to have XTree automatically replace existing files in the destination directory or No to have XTree prompt you before copying over a file with the same name.

Figure 4.17 shows the result of moving the NEW-VARS.BAT file. The left side of the screen was changed to an expanded file window so that all the files would appear.

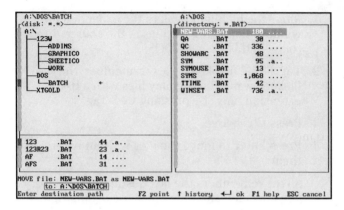

Fig. 4.16. The to: prompt enables you to specify the destination directory.

```
A:\DOS\BATCH                    A:\DOS
(directory: *.*)               (directory: *.BAT)
 123       .BAT      44 .a..    QA        .BAT       30 ....
 123R23    .BAT      23 .a..    QC        .BAT      336 ....
 AF        .BAT      14 ....    SHOWARC   .BAT       48 ....
 AFS       .BAT      31 ....    SYM       .BAT       95 .a..
 HOME      .BAT      43 .a..    SYMOUSE   .BAT       13 ....
 LET       .BAT      56 ....    SYMS      .BAT    1,068 ....
 NEW-VARS.BAT       180 ....    TTIME     .BAT       42 ....
                                WINSET    .BAT      736 .a..




FILE       Attributes  Copy  Delete  Edit  Filespec  Invert  Log disk  Move
COMMANDS   New date  Open  Print  Rename  Tag  Untag  View  eXecute  Quit
 tree   F7 autoview  F8 unsplit  F9 menu  F10 commands    F1 help  ESC cancel
```

Fig. 4.17. The result of moving the NEW-VARS.BAT file.

Moving Multiple Files

As you have seen in previous examples, XTree excels at multiple file operations. Moving multiple files in one step is no exception. To move the balance of the batch files, follow these steps:

1. Move the highlight back to the expanded file window displaying the files in the source directory—in this case, A:\DOS.

2. Tag all the displayed files (remember, the filespec was set to display files with a BAT extension only) by pressing Ctrl+Tag.

3. Press Ctrl+Move.

4. Press Enter to move the files without renaming them.

   XTree remembers the last destination directory you specified and offers it as the destination.

5. Press Enter to move the files.

Figure 4.18 shows the results of the move. When all the batch files were moved from the A:\DOS directory, the window changes back to a directory window and the message No Files Match appears in the small file window. If you used the Filespec command to change back to *.*, the window would again display files. The expanded file window showing the A:\DOS\BATCH directory displays all the moved files as soon as you make the window active.

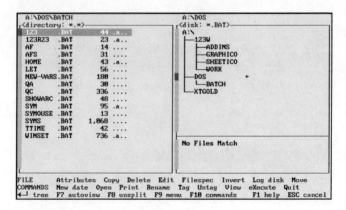

Fig. 4.18. The result of moving all the batch files to the A:\DOS\BATCH directory.

Deleting and Undeleting Files

XTree offers several methods of increasing disk space. You already have learned how to copy and move files. Chapter 5 covers archiving files— compressing them into libraries that require less than half their original space. In this section, you learn how to use XTree to efficiently delete files you no longer need.

Probably all PC users have accidentally erased a file or realized that an erased file really did contain useful data. Fortunately, DOS doesn't really erase files immediately, and you can use XTree to recover many files that you deleted in error.

NOTE   The capability to undelete files is an important enhancement in XTreeGold. This capability is not shared by XTree Easy or the older versions of XTree. As you read the sections on undeleting files, you might conclude that upgrading to XTreeGold, if only for its ability to undelete files, is worth the cost. For more information on the differences between XTreeGold and XTree Easy, see Chapter 2. Appendix B provides more information on the changes incorporated into XTree.

Deleting Single Files

Deleting a single file in XTree is simple; you select the file, select the Delete command, and answer Yes to confirm the deletion. As with the commands discussed earlier, you can only delete a single, selected file when a file window is active.

Before you delete the files, set the display to show a single-column display, because this type of display shows the date and time each file was last modified. The date and time information is particularly useful when you're deleting files; it can tell you which files are no longer in use and therefore are possible candidates for deletion.

To select and delete a file, follow these steps:

1. Highlight the file to delete—in this case, CACTUS.WK3.

2. From the drop-down File menu, select the Delete command. You also can select this command from the FILE COMMANDS menu.

3. Select Yes to confirm the deletion or No to cancel (see fig. 4.19).

```
Path: A:\123W\WORK                                    9-11-91  9:32:51 am

 3DAREA   .WK3    1,539 .a..   7-24-91  11:30:26 am   FILE *.*
 3DBAR    .WK3    1,539 .a..   7-24-91  11:10:48 am
 AUDITREE.WK3     1,172 .a..   6-19-91   6:10:18 pm   DISK  A:
 BACKTREE.WK3       851 .a..   6-19-91   5:48:20 pm    Available
 CACTUS   .WK3    2,989 .a..   6-11-89   9:04:52 am      Bytes       216,064
 CARDLIST.WK3     5,345 .a..   9-11-90   9:05:18 am
 CARDS    .WK3    3,929 .a..   8-07-91   3:37:40 pm   DIRECTORY Stats
 FREQTYPE.WK3    10,030 .a..   8-05-91   2:52:44 pm    Total
 FREQUENC.WK3     9,909 .a..   8-05-91   4:08:08 pm     Files            15
 FUNCTION.WK3     2,176 .a..   8-13-89   9:05:50 am     Bytes        61,225
 LEDGER   .WK3    2,766 .a..   8-27-91  12:30:16 pm    Matching
 SCANTYPE.WK3    10,054 .a..   3-01-89   9:07:00 am     Files            15
 SOLUTREE.WK3     1,892 .a..   6-26-91  11:46:32 am     Bytes        61,225
 VIEWTREE.WK3       843 .a..   6-19-91   6:19:26 pm    Tagged
 XYCHART  .WK3    6,191 .a..   9-10-89   9:06:26 am     Files             0
                                                       Bytes             0
                                                      Current File
                                                        CACTUS   .WK3
                                                        Bytes         2,989

DELETE file: CACTUS.WK3

Delete this file?                                Yes  No| F1 help  ESC cancel
```

Fig. 4.19. Select Yes to confirm the deletion or No to cancel it.

XTree deletes the file—in this case, CACTUS.WK3— and updates the file window display automatically.

Deleting Multiple Files

When you decide to clean the old files from your disk, you will probably decide to remove many files at the same time.

Refer to figure 4.19—the screen shows several old files that haven't been used for quite some time. In deciding which old files to delete, you determine that any file that hasn't been used in over a year will go. Figure 4.20 shows four files that meet this criteria (these files were tagged using the Tag command).

```
Path: A:\123W\WORK                              9-11-91  9:46:06 am

 3DAREA  .WK3    1,539 .a..  7-24-91 11:30:26 am  FILE  *.*
 3DBAR   .WK3    1,539 .a..  7-24-91 11:10:48 am
 AUDITREE.WK3    1,172 .a..  6-19-91  6:10:18 pm  DISK  A:
 BACKTREE.WK3      851 .a..  6-19-91  5:48:20 pm  Available
 CARDLIST.WK3◆   5,345 .a..  9-11-90  9:05:18 am    Bytes       219,136
 CARDS   .WK3    3,929 .a..  8-07-91  3:37:40 pm
 FREQTYPE.WK3   10,030 .a..  8-05-91  2:52:44 pm  DIRECTORY Stats
 FREQUENC.WK3    9,909 .a..  8-05-91  4:08:08 pm  Total
 FUNCTION.WK3◆   2,176 .a..  8-13-89  9:05:50 am    Files            14
 LEDGER  .WK3    2,766 .a..  8-27-91 12:30:16 pm    Bytes        58,236
 SCANTYPE.WK3◆  10,054 .a..  3-01-89  9:07:00 am  Matching
 SOLVTREE.WK3    1,892 .a..  6-26-91 11:46:32 am    Files            14
 VIEWTREE.WK3      843 .a..  6-19-91  6:19:26 pm    Bytes        58,236
 XYCHART .WK3◆   6,191 .a..  9-10-89  9:06:26 am  Tagged
                                                   Files             4
                                                   Bytes        23,766
                                                 Current File
                                                   XYCHART .WK3
                                                   Bytes         6,191

FILE       Attributes  Copy  Delete  Edit  Filespec  Invert  Log disk  Move
COMMANDS   New date  Open  Print  Rename  Tag  Untag  View  eXecute  Quit
◄┘ tree  F7 autoview  F8 split    F9 menu  F10 commands    F1 help  ESC cancel
```

Fig. 4.20. Four files tagged for deletion.

To delete multiple files, follow these steps:

1. Tag the files to be deleted. You can use any of XTree's tagging methods discussed earlier to tag the files.

2. From the Tagged drop-down menu, select Delete. You also press Ctrl+Delete to select the command.

3. Select **Y**es to confirm the deletion of each file or **N**o to proceed without further confirmation.

XTree deletes the files and updates the display. Notice that figure 4.21 no longer shows the deleted files.

```
 Path: A:\123W\WORK                                 9-11-91   9:55:57 am

 3DAREA  .WK3    1,539 .a.. 7-24-91 11:30:26 am     FILE  *.*
 3DBAR   .WK3    1,539 .a.. 7-24-91 11:10:48 am
 AUDITREE.WK3    1,172 .a.. 6-19-91  6:10:18 pm     DISK  A:
 BACKTREE.WK3      851 .a.. 6-19-91  5:48:28 pm     Available
 CARDS   .WK3    3,929 .a.. 8-07-91  3:37:40 pm       Bytes      244,224
 FREQTYPE.WK3   10,030 .a.. 8-05-91  2:52:44 pm
 FREQUENC.WK3    9,989 .a.. 8-05-91  4:08:08 pm     DIRECTORY Stats
 LEDGER  .WK3    2,766 .a.. 8-27-91 12:30:16 pm     Total
 SOLVTREE.WK3    1,892 .a.. 6-26-91 11:46:32 am       Files           10
 VIEWTREE.WK3      843 .a.. 6-19-91  6:19:26 pm       Bytes       34,470
                                                    Matching
                                                      Files           10
                                                      Bytes       34,470
                                                    Tagged
                                                      Files            0
                                                      Bytes            0
                                                    Current File
                                                      3DAREA  .WK3
                                                      Bytes        1,539

FILE         Attributes  Copy  Delete  Edit  Filespec  Invert  Log disk  Move
COMMANDS     New date  Open  Print  Rename  Tag  Untag  View  eXecute  Quit
↵ tree   F7 autoview   F8 split   F9 menu   F10 commands   F1 help  ESC cancel
```

Fig. 4.21. The deleted files no longer appear in the display.

Undeleting Files

Deleting or erasing files seems so permanent that people often are surprised to learn that they can sometimes recover deleted files. If a file is gone, it's gone forever, isn't it? How can you bring back a file after it was erased?

Actually, part of the problem is the terminology. Deleted files are not actually erased.

When you delete a file, it is no longer included in the list of files on the disk, and the space it occupied is no longer included in the list of used space. The file still exists until its space is given to another file. Because DOS no longer includes it in the list of files, however, you cannot use the file. XTree can find deleted files and recover them—provided that another file hasn't already reused the deleted file's space.

Imagine that after deleting the worksheet files in the previous example, someone called you to ask for a copy of FUNCTION.WK3. Upon receiving this call, you remembered that the worksheet was really a master template. Whenever someone used the file, they modified it for their purposes, and then saved it and their data using a new file name. Unless you want to recreate the master template, undeleting the file seems like your best recourse.

XTree's undelete command is called Oops!, and it is only available when a directory window is active. Although this setup might seem confusing, especially because you want to undelete a file, remember that file windows only work with files they can display in a file list. Because the file list no longer includes deleted files, you must use the directory window instead.

To undelete an accidentally deleted file—in this case, FUNCTION.WK3—follow these steps:

1. Press **Enter** once or twice, as needed, to make the directory window active. Be sure that the directory containing the deleted files is high-lighted. In this case, A:\123W\WORK is highlighted.

2. Select the Oops! command from either the DIR COMMANDS menu or the drop-down File menu.

   After you select the Oops! command, XTree scans the highlighted directory to find any de-leted files. After the scan is completed, the de-leted files appear on-screen. Notice that the first character of each file's name is replaced with a question mark (?). When files are deleted, DOS replaces the first character of the file name with a special character to indicate deleted files. No record of the original character remains, so XTree displays a question mark to indicate that you must supply the first character of the file name when you undelete the file.

The file attributes also do not appear. In their place, XTree uses the following notations:

Notation	Function
....	Indicates that you probably can recover the file successfully.
.**.	Indicates that you should recover this file first (or you might not be able to recover the file).
????	Indicates that you probably cannot recover the file because another file might have used some or all of its disk space.

In figure 4.22, the first file ?ACTUS.WK3 shows .**. and the rest of the files show .... .

```
 Path: A:\123W\WORK                              9-11-91 10:35:48 am

 ?ACTUS   .WK3     2,989  .**.   6-11-89   9:04:52 am    FILE  *.*
 ?ARDLIST.WK3      5,345  ....   9-11-90   9:05:18 am
 ?UNCTION.WK3      2,176  ....   8-13-89   9:05:50 am    DISK  A:
 ?CANTYPE.WK3     10,054  ....   3-01-89   9:07:00 am    Available
 ?YCHART .WK3      6,191  ....   9-10-89   9:06:26 am       Bytes      244,224

                                                        UNDELETE Stats
                                                         Total
                                                          Files          5

                                                         Matching
                                                          Files          5

                                                         Conflicting
                                                          Files          0

                                                         Current File
                                                          ?ACTUS  .WK3
                                                          Bytes      2,989

 UNDELETE   Undelete  Sort criteria
 COMMANDS
                                                        F1 help  ESC exit
```

Fig. 4.22. Files to be undeleted.

3. Highlight the file you want to recover—in this case, highlight ?UNCTION.WK3.

4. Select **U**ndelete and type the file name. In this example, you would type **FUNCTION.WK3** (see fig. 4.23).

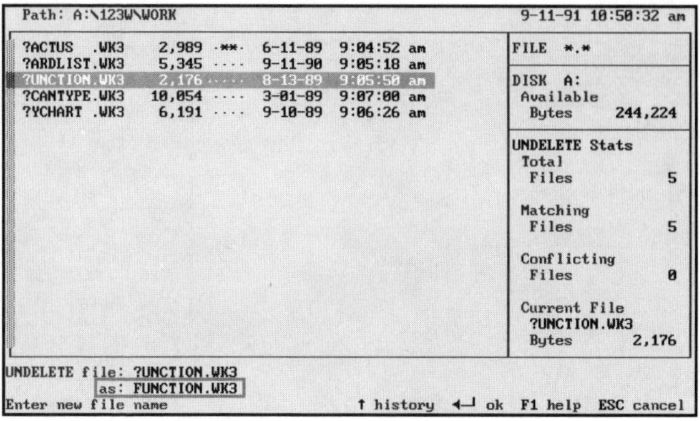

Fig. 4.23. File name specified as FUNCTION.WK3.

XTree then attempts to recover the file and reports whether the attempt was successful. The
Undelete window reappears. Figure 4.24 shows,
however, that only three deleted files now remain, instead of the four you probably expected.
Although five deleted files appeared originally,
undeleting a file used the first available space
in the directory listing—the space formerly
occupied by ?ACTUS.WK3. As you can see,
?ACTUS.WK3 is no longer listed and cannot be
undeleted.

Press Esc to return to the directory window, and
then press Enter twice to display the expanded
file window.

Erasing Files Permanently

Sometimes actually erasing deleted files is important.
You wouldn't want someone to undelete files contain-
ing your confidential business plans, for example.
Whatever your reason, it can be reassuring to know
XTree can do what DOS cannot—remove deleted files
permanently.

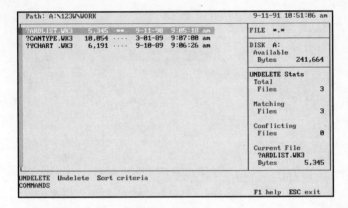

Fig. 4.24. Only three deleted files remain for undeletion.

Because the **W**ash disk command absolutely prevents deleted files from being undeleted, XTree requires you to confirm the command. The **W**ash deleted space command is available on the directory window drop-down Volume menu. The **W**ash disk command is available on the ALT DIR COMMANDS menu.

After you select the **W**ash deleted space or **W**ash disk command, XTree enables you to select a single-pass or six-pass overwrite of the deleted space by pressing **F2** to toggle between the two methods. Both methods meet the U.S. government DoD 5220.22-M standard for overwriting classified data, but the six-pass overwrite goes over the deleted space six times—writing ones the first time, then zeros, and alternating until the space has been overwritten six times.

You can check to see that the deleted files have really been erased by again selecting the **O**ops! command. The same deleted files are still listed and XTree will undelete them at your request. The undeleted files, however, will not contain any data—their data was overwritten.

Renaming Files

You might want to rename files for several reasons. The XTree commands for renaming files function much like several other file management commands presented earlier in this chapter. First, a file window must be active; second, renaming more than one file with a single command requires tagging the files before executing the command.

Suppose that you have a group of word processing files that were saved using a TXT extension. To make them appear automatically when you use your word processor's File Open command, however, you must change their extensions to DOC.

To change file extensions, follow these steps:

1. Highlight the directory containing the files to be renamed. In this example, highlight B:\WP\DOCS.

2. Press Enter to make the file window active.

3. Press Ctrl+Tag to tag all the files in the window. (Use the Filespec command first to limit the range of files displayed in the window.)

4. Press Ctrl+Rename to rename the tagged files. XTree responds with the prompt RENAME all tagged files to. This prompt asks how you want to rename the tagged files (see fig. 4.25).

5. Enter the pattern for renaming the files—in this example, *.DOC—and press Enter.

XTree renames the files and updates the display to show the new file names. If you attempt to rename a file using a name that would duplicate an existing file name, XTree responds that it is unable to rename the file. In most cases, you can avoid this problem by the careful use of wild cards. If XTree is unable to rename one or more files due to name conflicts, either reissue the command using a different wild card pattern or rename the files individually.

```
Path: B:\WP\DOCS                              9-11-91  3:32:47 pm

 B:\                                   FILE  *.*
   ├─DOS
   └─WP                                DISK  B:APPS_WRITE
       └─DOCS           ←              Available
                                         Bytes    1,144,832

                                       DIRECTORY Stats
                                         Total
                                           Files              4
                                           Bytes         38,712
                                         Matching
                                           Files              4
                                           Bytes         38,712
                                         Tagged
 ATREE    .TXT◆    176 .a..  8-29-91  5:53:36 pm    Files              4
 BIO      .TXT◆  4,096 ....  7-02-91 10:05:32 am    Bytes         38,712
 CLASSOUT .TXT◆ 14,839 .a..  8-08-91 12:44:00 pm  Current File
 CPATALK  .TXT◆ 19,601 .a..  8-07-91 10:24:08 am    ATREE    .TXT
                                                    Bytes            176
RENAME all tagged files
         to: *.DOC
Enter file specification              ↑ history  ←┘ ok  F1 help  ESC cancel
```

Fig. 4.25. Specifying the new name for tagged files.

Editing Files

DOS batch files are simple text files that enter the
commands to run programs or execute other functions just as you would if you were typing the commands at the keyboard. At times, you might need to
make a change in a batch file or other text file, and
XTree provides an easy way to make such a change.
In this section, you will see how to use the XTree
1Word text editor to edit a simple batch file.

The 1Word text editor is a simple editor. It does not
support a mouse, and certainly is not a substitute for
a word processor. On the other hand, 1Word is a
good substitute for EDLIN, the DOS text editor that
many people use to modify batch files and other
simple text files.

1Word is available when either directory or file windows are active. If a file window is active when you
select **E**dit, 1Word offers to edit the currently highlighted file if it is a text file. If the highlighted file is
not a text file, an error message appears telling you
that 1Word cannot edit nontext files. If a directory
window is active when you select the command,
XTree prompts you to enter the name of a file to edit.

Suppose that you want to make a small change
in the batch file 123.BAT, which is located in the
A:\DOS\BATCH directory. To start the 1Word editor
and load 123.BAT for editing, follow these steps:

1. Highlight the directory that contains the file you
    want to change. For this example, highlight the
    A:\DOS\BATCH directory.

2. In the file window, highlight the file to edit—in
    this example, 123.BAT.

3. From the File drop-down menu, select Edit. You
    also can select Edit from the FILE COMMANDS
    menu.

4. Press Enter to accept the highlighted file
    (123.BAT) as the file to edit. If the correct file
    name does not appear as the file to edit, correct
    the name before you press Enter.

Figure 4.26 shows the 1Word screen after loading
123.BAT.

```
┌──────────────────────────────────────Esc cancel──────┐
│ A:\DOS\BATCH\123.BAT                  Size    51  1:41:37│
│ Ins Hard          Num AskFrwd    Line   1 Col 1  Byte    1  9-11-91│
├───────────────────────────────────────────────────────┤
│@ECHO OFF                                               │
│MOUSE                                                   │
│C:                                                     │
│CD \123R3                                              │
│123                                                    │
│CD \                                                   │
│CLS                                                    │
│                                                        │
│                                                        │
│                                                        │
│                                                        │
│                                                        │
│                                                        │
│                                                        │
│                                                        │
│                                                        │
└────────────────────────────────────────────────────────┘
```

Fig. 4.26. Editing 123.BAT with 1Word.

Because 1Word is a screen editor, you can use
the arrow keys to move the cursor to any line on the
screen and make changes. When you start 1Word,

it displays a block cursor to indicate that the editor is in Insert mode. That is, anything you type is added to the line and existing text moves to the right. If you press the Ins key, the cursor changes to an underline, which indicates that the editor is now in Overtype mode. In this mode, anything you type replaces existing text.

1Word uses the Ctrl key, in combination with other keys, to perform many of its functions. Chapter 8 includes a command reference of 1Word commands.

In this example, suppose that you moved your 1-2-3 program files from the C: drive to the D: drive. 1Word enables you to make this change quickly. Looking at figure 4.26, you can see that line 3 of 123.BAT makes the C: drive current. You also can see the word Ins (for insert mode) on the left side of the status line, just below the name of the file being edited. To make this change to the file, follow these steps:

1. Press the Ins key so that the mode indicator changes to Ovr. In overwrite mode, any characters you type replace existing characters.

2. Move the cursor down to the character to change and enter the replacement text. In this example, move the cursor to the first character of line 3 and enter D.

3. Because no other changes are necessary, press Esc; then press Enter to select Save file and quit. You return to XTree.

1Word saves a copy of the original text file with the same name, but it uses BAK as the file extension.

The 1Word text editor is just right for making changes to small text files such as the batch file in this example. For more information on using 1Word, refer to Chapter 8.

Summary

This chapter covered the most common file management functions with XTree. These functions, which include copying, moving, deleting, renaming, and editing files are important to every PC user. Chapter 5 expands on file management and shows you more advanced file management functions.

Performing Advanced File Management

C hapter 4 introduced you to basic file management tasks. This chapter expands on file management by examining the more advanced file management functions that you can perform with XTree.

Before continuing with the tasks in this chapter, you should be familiar with the basic skills covered in Chapter 4. By now, you should have a clear understanding of tagging and untagging files. Also, you should be comfortable using either the drop-down menus or the menus at the bottom of the screen. In addition, you should be able to decide when to use commands that affect a single file and when to use commands that affect tagged files. In this chapter, you will see a more streamlined approach toward each task. Instead of repeating the steps involved in the basic setup for a task, for example, these steps simply tell you to "tag the desired files."

Sorting Files

When you use the DIR command in DOS, files appear in an unsorted order. Usually, the newest files appear at the end of the list. If you delete files from a directory, however, files added later might appear at the location of the deleted files instead of at the end of the list.

XTree, on the other hand, sorts the file listing before displaying it. By default, XTree sorts the listing in alphabetical order by the file name. If you prefer, however, you can select another sort criteria.

NOTE Unlike some other utility programs, XTree does not change the order of the DOS directory listing. When you leave XTree, the DIR command shows the same unsorted listing. XTree's sorting applies only as long as you are actually using XTree.

Figure 5.1 shows a typical XTree sorted file listing displayed in an expanded file window.

```
Path: A:\DOS                                    9-12-91  1:17:19 pm

ADAPTEC .ZIP     1,098 .a..   1-30-91 12:32:24 pm   FILE  *.*
APPEND  .EXE    10,774 ....   4-09-91  5:00:00 am
ARCE    .COM     7,128 ....   8-14-89  4:43:16 pm   DISK  A:
ASCII   .EXE     9,914 ....   3-27-87 12:48:46 pm   Available
ASSIGN  .COM     6,399 ....   4-09-91  5:00:00 am     Bytes      211,968
ATPERF  .EXE    95,924 ....   1-23-87  2:51:26 pm
ATTRIB  .EXE    15,796 ....   4-09-91  5:00:00 am   DIRECTORY Stats
BACKUP  .EXE    36,092 ....   4-09-91  5:00:00 am   Total
BOOTWARM.COM        16 ....   4-21-86 11:02:24 am     Files           46
BYTEDUMP.EXE    24,825 ....   5-17-90  4:24:04 pm     Bytes      624,374
CHKDSK  .EXE    16,200 ....   4-09-91  5:00:00 am   Matching
CLR     .COM        79 .a..   6-29-88  1:00:00 pm     Files           46
CPANEL  .COM    19,858 ....   8-01-88 12:00:02 am     Bytes      624,374
DEL     .COM     1,152 ....   2-12-84 11:58:52 am   Tagged
DISKCOPY.COM    11,793 ....   4-09-91  5:00:00 am     Files            0
DISKMANY.COM     4,329 ....   7-26-90  2:15:34 pm     Bytes            0
DISPLAY .SYS    15,792 ....   4-09-91  5:00:00 am   Current File
DOSKEY  .COM     5,883 .a..   4-09-91  5:00:00 am     ADAPTEC .ZIP
DR      .COM     3,370 ....   8-27-87 10:21:42 am     Bytes        1,098

FILE        Attributes  Copy  Delete  Edit  Filespec  Invert  Log disk  Move
COMMANDS    New date  Open  Print  Rename  Tag  Untag  View  eXecute  Quit
◄┘ tree    F7 autoview   F8 split    F9 menu   F10 commands   F1 help   ESC cancel
```

Fig. 5.1. By default, XTree sorts file listings in alphabetical order by file name.

Normally, the default sort order works well, and it certainly is easier to use than the jumbled list that DOS presents. You might prefer another sort order, however.

Changing the File Display Sort Order

You can change XTree's file display sort order whether the active window is a directory window or a file window. Because the sort order changes the way that all files appear, the new sort order setting does not use file tags. All displayed files, tagged or not, appear in the new sort order. Remember, however, that the Filespec command controls which files appear. Changing the sort order does not change the FILE setting.

To change the XTree file display sort setting, follow these steps:

1. From the Window drop-down menu, select Sort criteria. You also can press Alt+S.

2. Select one of the following options:

Option	Function
Order	Select first to toggle the sort order from ascending to descending or descending to ascending order.
Path Yes	Select first to group files in branch, showall, and global windows by directory.
Path No	Select first to show files in branch, showall, and global windows without regard to directories.
Name	Sorts the file display alphabetically by file name; this is the XTree default sort order.

Option	Function
Extension	Sorts the file display first in order by file extension, and then by file name within each group of extensions.
Date	Sorts the file display first in order by file date and time, and then by file name, if dates and times are the same.
Size	Sorts the file display first in order by file size, and then by file name, if sizes are the same.
Unsort	Displays files unsorted according to their position in the DOS directory listing. This is the order in which DOS commands process groups of files.

Figures 5.2 through 5.5 show the results of changing XTree's file display sort order.

```
 Path: A:\DOS                                          9-12-91  1:38:19 pm
┌─────────────────────────────────────────┐ ┌──────────────────────────────┐
│ ARCE     .COM    7,128 ....  8-14-89  4:43:16 pm│ FILE  *.*                │
│ ASSIGN   .COM    6,399 ....  4-09-91  5:00:00 am│                          │
│ BOOTWARM.COM        16 ....  4-21-86 11:02:24 am│ DISK A:                  │
│ CLR      .COM       79 .a..  6-29-88  1:00:00 pm│ Available                │
│ CPANEL   .COM   19,858 ....  8-01-88 12:00:02 am│   Bytes          211,968 │
│ DEL      .COM    1,152 ....  2-12-84 11:50:52 am│                          │
│ DISKCOPY.COM    11,793 ....  4-09-91  5:00:00 am│ DIRECTORY Stats          │
│ DISKMANY.COM     4,329 ....  7-26-90  2:15:34 pm│ Total                    │
│ DOSKEY   .COM    5,883 .a..  4-09-91  5:00:00 am│   Files               46 │
│ DR       .COM    3,370 ....  8-27-87 10:21:42 am│   Bytes          624,374 │
│ DU       .COM    1,788 ....  6-29-88  1:00:00 pm│ Matching                 │
│ ESU      .COM    8,974 ....  6-29-88  1:00:00 pm│   Files               46 │
│ FORMAT   .COM   32,911 ....  4-09-91  5:00:00 am│   Bytes          624,374 │
│ MENU     .COM    2,540 ....  8-01-88 12:00:02 am│ Tagged                   │
│ MORE     .COM    2,618 .a..  4-09-91  5:00:00 am│   Files                0 │
│ MOUSE    .COM   31,833 ....  6-07-90  2:24:00 am│   Bytes                0 │
│ ROMDATE  .COM      148 ....  6-29-88  1:00:00 pm│ Current File             │
│ SHIP     .COM      912 ....  1-12-87 10:24:44 am│   ARCE     .COM          │
│ TREE     .COM    6,901 ....  4-09-91  5:00:00 am│   Bytes            7,128 │
└─────────────────────────────────────────┘ └──────────────────────────────┘
 FILE        Attributes Copy Delete Edit Filespec Invert Log disk  Move
 COMMANDS    New date Open Print Rename Tag Untag View  eXecute Quit
 ◄┘ tree  F7 autoview  F8 split   F9 menu  F10 commands   F1 help  ESC cancel
```

Fig. 5.2. Files sorted by extension.

Although XTree does not physically rearrange files on the disk according to the specified sort order, it does process commands in the order in which files appear. If, for example, you sort files in descending order by size, tag the files, and then use the Ctrl+Copy command, the files are copied to the new directory or disk in the specified sort order—largest files first,

followed by smaller ones. If you use the XTree default
sort order, files are copied sorted by name. As long as
the new directory or disk was empty before the copy,
even the DOS directory listing will show the files in
the same sorted order. If you are copying files to a
directory that already contains files, however, the
files might appear differently.

```
 Path: A:\DOS                                    9-12-91  1:38:45 pm
┌─────────────────────────────────────────────┬─────────────────────┐
│ DEL      .COM    1,152 ....  2-12-04 11:50:52 am │ FILE  *.*        │
│ BOOTWARM.COM        16 ....  4-21-86 11:02:24 am │                  │
│ SHIP     .COM       912 ....  1-12-87 10:24:44 am │ DISK  A:          │
│ ATPERF   .EXE   95,924 ....  1-23-87  2:51:26 pm │ Available          │
│ ASCII    .EXE    9,914 ....  3-27-87 12:48:46 pm │   Bytes    211,968 │
│ DR       .COM    3,370 ....  8-27-87 10:21:42 am │                    │
│ EXEMOD   .EXE   11,765 .a..  2-01-88  1:00:00 pm │ DIRECTORY Stats    │
│ ZSPOOL   .COM    3,004 ....  4-06-88  3:16:18 pm │ Total              │
│ CLR      .COM       79 .a..  6-29-88  1:00:00 pm │   Files         46 │
│ DU       .COM    1,788 ....  6-29-88  1:00:00 pm │   Bytes    624,374 │
│ ESU      .COM    8,974 ....  6-29-88  1:00:00 pm │ Matching           │
│ ROMDATE  .COM      148 ....  6-29-88  1:00:00 pm │   Files         46 │
│ CPANEL   .COM   19,858 ....  8-01-88 12:00:02 am │   Bytes    624,374 │
│ MENU     .COM    2,540 ....  8-01-88 12:00:02 am │ Tagged             │
│ ARCE     .COM    7,128 ....  8-14-89  4:43:16 pm │   Files          0 │
│ HEXDUMP  .EXE   26,249 .... 11-10-89 10:56:02 am │   Bytes          0 │
│ BYTEDUMP .EXE   24,825 ....  5-17-90  4:24:04 pm │ Current File       │
│ MOUSE    .COM   31,833 ....  6-07-90  2:24:00 am │   DEL      .COM    │
│ DISKMANY .COM    4,329 ....  7-26-90  2:15:34 pm │   Bytes      1,152 │
├─────────────────────────────────────────────┴─────────────────────┤
│ FILE      Attributes Copy Delete Edit Filespec Invert Log disk Move │
│ COMMANDS  New date Open Print Rename Tag Untag View  eXecute Quit    │
│ ←┘ tree  F7 autoview  F8 split    F9 menu  F10 commands   F1 help  ESC cancel │
└───────────────────────────────────────────────────────────────────┘
```

Fig. 5.3. Files sorted by date.

```
 Path: A:\DOS                                    9-12-91  2:02:28 pm
┌─────────────────────────────────────────────┬─────────────────────┐
│ ATPERF   .EXE   95,924 ....  1-23-87  2:51:26 pm │ FILE  *.*        │
│ MEM      .EXE   39,818 ....  4-09-91  5:00:00 am │                  │
│ BACKUP   .EXE   36,092 ....  4-09-91  5:00:00 am │ DISK  A:          │
│ FORMAT   .COM   32,911 ....  4-09-91  5:00:00 am │ Available          │
│ MOUSE    .COM   31,833 ....  6-07-90  2:24:00 am │   Bytes    211,968 │
│ HEXDUMP  .EXE   26,249 .... 11-10-89 10:56:02 am │                    │
│ BYTEDUMP .EXE   24,825 ....  5-17-90  4:24:04 pm │ DIRECTORY Stats    │
│ REPLACE  .EXE   20,226 .a..  4-09-91  5:00:00 am │ Total              │
│ CPANEL   .COM   19,858 ....  8-01-88 12:00:02 am │   Files         46 │
│ FC       .EXE   18,650 ....  4-09-91  5:00:00 am │   Bytes    624,374 │
│ JOIN     .EXE   17,870 ....  4-09-91  5:00:00 am │ Matching           │
│ CHKDSK   .EXE   16,200 ....  4-09-91  5:00:00 am │   Files         46 │
│ XCOPY    .EXE   15,804 .a..  4-09-91  5:00:00 am │   Bytes    624,374 │
│ ATTRIB   .EXE   15,796 ....  4-09-91  5:00:00 am │ Tagged             │
│ DISPLAY  .SYS   15,792 ....  4-09-91  5:00:00 am │   Files          0 │
│ EDLIN    .EXE   12,642 ....  4-09-91  5:00:00 am │   Bytes          0 │
│ FASTOPEN.EXE    12,050 ....  4-09-91  5:00:00 am │ Current File       │
│ SETVER   .EXE   12,007 .a..  4-09-91  5:00:00 am │   ATPERF   .EXE    │
│ DISKCOPY.COM    11,793 ....  4-09-91  5:00:00 am │   Bytes     95,924 │
├─────────────────────────────────────────────┴─────────────────────┤
│ FILE      Attributes Copy Delete Edit  Filespec Invert Log disk Move │
│ COMMANDS  New date Open Print Rename Tag Untag View  eXecute Quit    │
│ ←┘ tree  F7 autoview  F8 split    F9 menu  F10 commands   F1 help  ESC cancel │
└───────────────────────────────────────────────────────────────────┘
```

Fig. 5.4. Files sorted in descending size order.

```
Path: A:\DOS                                          9-12-91  2:03:00 pm
 APPEND    .EXE    10,774  ....   4-09-91   5:00:00 am   FILE  *.*
 ATTRIB    .EXE    15,796  ....   4-09-91   5:00:00 am
 BACKUP    .EXE    36,092  ....   4-09-91   5:00:00 am   DISK A:
 CHKDSK    .EXE    16,200  ....   4-09-91   5:00:00 am    Available
 EDLIN     .EXE    12,642  ....   4-09-91   5:00:00 am      Bytes       211,968
 FASTOPEN  .EXE    12,050  ....   4-09-91   5:00:00 am
 FC        .EXE    18,650  ....   4-09-91   5:00:00 am   DIRECTORY Stats
 FIND      .EXE     6,770  ....   4-09-91   5:00:00 am    Total
 JOIN      .EXE    17,870  ....   4-09-91   5:00:00 am     Files           46
 LABEL     .EXE     9,390  ....   4-09-91   5:00:00 am     Bytes      624,374
 MEM       .EXE    39,818  ....   4-09-91   5:00:00 am    Matching
 REPLACE   .EXE    20,226  .a..   4-09-91   5:00:00 am     Files           46
 SETVER    .EXE    12,007  .a..   4-09-91   5:00:00 am     Bytes      624,374
 SHARE     .EXE    10,912  ....   4-09-91   5:00:00 am    Tagged
 SORT      .EXE     6,938  ....   4-09-91   5:00:00 am     Files            0
 XCOPY     .EXE    15,804  .a..   4-09-91   5:00:00 am     Bytes            0
 ASSIGN    .COM     6,399  ....   4-09-91   5:00:00 am    Current File
 DISKCOPY  .COM    11,793  ....   4-09-91   5:00:00 am     APPEND   .EXE
 DISPLAY   .SYS    15,792  ....   4-09-91   5:00:00 am     Bytes       10,774

FILE       Attributes  Copy  Delete  Edit  Filespec  Invert  Log disk  Move
COMMANDS   New date  Open  Print  Rename  Tag  Untag  View  eXecute  Quit
←┘ tree   F7 autoview  F8 split    F9 menu   F10 commands   F1 help  ESC cancel
```

Fig. 5.5. Files displayed in unsorted DOS directory order.

Reducing File Fragmentation

Over a period of time, as you use your hard disk, files can become fragmented. *Fragmented* means that they are not stored in one contiguous area, but are separated into two or more pieces. The more fragmented your files become, the longer the time necessary to read files from your hard disk. Although XTree wasn't designed to reduce file fragmentation, in many cases it can do just that.

The main reason files become fragmented is because of the way DOS reuses space previously allocated to deleted files. If you delete several small files on a disk, the disk will probably have several nonadjacent spaces available the next time you store a large file. When DOS allocates file space, it uses the available space until no more space is remaining in the current piece; then it uses another piece. After a time, you might have plenty of disk space available, but that space might consist of many small pieces. When you save a large file, the file is fragmented.

You often can reduce file fragmentation by moving files to another disk and then copying them back—largest files first. Although this method is not as certain to eliminate fragmentation as a utility designed for the purpose, you still can achieve useful results. If you want to try using XTree to reduce file fragmentation, use the following procedure:

1. Change the sort order to descending by size.

2. Tag the files.

3. Press Ctrl+Move to move the files to another disk. You must use Move—not Copy—to free up the disk space.

4. Copy the files back using the same sort order—descending by size.

If you move your files from your hard disk to diskettes, be sure to number the diskettes so that you can copy the files back in the correct order.

Although you probably will find some improvement, especially if your hard disk is badly fragmented, remember that XTree wasn't designed to unfragment your hard disk. Utility programs that have functions designed to unfragment your hard disk, such as the Norton Utilities, do a faster and more thorough job.

Comparing Files

XTree also can easily find and compare all files with duplicate file names anywhere on your computer.

XTree does not compare the contents of files. Instead, it compares directory information about identically named files. You can view each file's location, size, attributes, and date and time of creation or modification. If two files have the same size, attributes, date, and time, you probably can assume that the files are identical.

Because XTree compares files that have the same names and extensions, the files being compared must be in different directories. DOS does not allow files in the same directory to share the same file name and extension.

XTree can compare the files in two specific directories (such as A:\DOS and C:\DOS), or it can compare files in a broader range. If you want to compare the files in two specific directories, you use the directory window Compare command. Comparing a broader range of files requires that you first make a branch, showall, or global file window active, and then use the Alt+F4 command. The two commands are similar, although the directory window command automatically tags files that meet your specified criteria. The branch, showall, or global file window command, on the other hand, simply displays the files that match. The following section covers the directory window Compare command, and the section following it examines the branch, showall, or global file window Alt+F4 compare command.

Comparing Files in Two Specified Directories

To compare the duplicate file names in two specific directories, follow these steps:

1. Highlight the first directory in a directory window. The Compare command tags those files in the current directory that match your specified comparison criteria. Unless you intend to manipulate these files in addition to any currently tagged files, use the Untag command to remove any current file tags before you begin.

2. Select Compare. XTree then prompts you for the second directory.

3. Enter the name of the second directory. If you have used the Compare command previously, you can use ↑ or the mouse to select the command history. You can select a previously entered directory from the command history by highlighting it and pressing Enter. Press Enter to continue.

4. Select the comparison criteria (see fig. 5.6). You can choose any combination of the following:

Option	Function
Identical	Tags files in the current directory that have the same name and date as a file in the second directory.
Unique	Tags any files in the current directory that do not have the same name as a file in the second directory.
Newer	Tags files in the current directory that have a more recent date and the same name as a file in the second directory.
Older	Tags files in the current directory that have an older date and the same name as a file in the second directory.

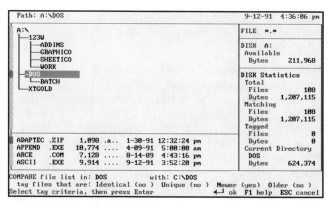

Fig. 5.6. Selecting the comparison criteria.

Each time you select one of the criteria, the criteria toggles from yes to no or no to yes.

5. When you finish selecting the comparison criteria, press Enter to continue.

When deciding on comparison criteria, don't be confused by the effects of the options. Suppose that you select both Identical and Newer. XTree would then tag any files in the current directory that have the same or a more recent date than files with the same names in the second directory. Using this selection would make it impossible to tell which files had an identical date and which ones were newer.

Comparing Files in More Than Two Directories

If you want to compare file lists in a broader range of directories for identically named files, you must use the branch, showall, or global file window Alt+F4 compare command. Unlike the directory window Compare command, Alt+F4 shows you the name and path of each matching file, instead of automatically tagging the matching files in one directory. If you want to tag the files in the resulting list, you can do so after you use Alt+F4.

When you compare file lists using the Alt+F4 compare command, the default display might appear to be exactly like any other branch, showall, or global file list. If you look at the display more closely, however, you will see that every file displayed is a duplicate. Like the directory window Compare command, you have several options for changing which files actually appear. You can decide to view only file names that are not duplicated; you can choose to view duplicated file names regardless of date or only if their dates match; or you can view the newest or the oldest version of each file. In addition, you can specify whether to ignore the locations of files, only show duplicates on different drives, or only show duplicates on different drives with the same path names.

Before using the Alt+F4 compare command, decide on the range of directories to be compared. If you only want to compare files on one branch of the directory tree for one disk, make a branch file window active. This choice might be appropriate if you want to compare the contents of several data directories that were subdirectories of a program directory. Remember, you can further limit the range of files compared by using the Filespec command.

If you want to find duplicates on the entire space of your hard disk, first make a showall file window active. The Alt+F4 compare command would then compare the contents of all the directories on the disk. You also can use the Filespec command to limit the range of files compared in this case, as well. The showall file window is a good choice when you want to limit the amount of wasted space on your hard disk by finding and deleting unneeded duplicate files.

Finally, if you want to find duplicates on any logged disk, use a global file window. The window includes any disk that XTree has read. If you use a global file window, the Scope option becomes available, and you can require that displayed matching files be on separate disks. A global file window is effective when you need to find the latest versions of files, but you aren't sure which disk contains them.

After you decide which type of file window is appropriate for a particular file list comparison, follow these steps to use the Alt+F4 compare command:

1. If you will be using a branch file window, highlight the parent directory of the directories you want to compare.

NOTE The highlighted parent directory should not be the root directory. If you select the Branch command while the root directory is highlighted, the branch file window is identical to a showall file window—all directories are subdirectories of the root directory.

2. If you want to use a wild card to limit the range of files to be compared, use the Filespec command to enter the appropriate wild card filespec.

3. With a directory window active, select Branch, Showall, or Global to activate the type of file window for the comparison.

4. Press Alt+F4 to initiate the compare command. XTree displays the comparison criteria at the bottom of the screen. The Scope option is only available if a global file window is active.

You can select one of the comparison options from the following list:

Option	Function
Duplicate name	Displays files that have duplicate file names, regardless of their dates.
Unique name	Displays only files that are not duplicates.
Identical dates	Displays duplicate file names only if the files have the same dates.
Newest Date	Displays the newest version of any duplicate file names.
Oldest date	Displays the oldest version of any duplicate file names.

If a global file window is active, you can select the
Scope command. Selecting this command switches
the range of files between all (ignores file location),
across drives (matching files must be on different
disks), and matching paths (matching files must be in
the same directory paths but on different disks). You
can select the Scope command as needed until the
correct range is included; selecting any of the other
comparison criteria executes the compare command.

Figure 5.7 shows the result of the Alt+F4 compare
command when a global file window is active, the
scope is all, and the Duplicate comparison criteria
was selected. Notice that all files shown are duplicates.

Using the file list comparison in figure 5.7, you can
step down through the list and tag duplicate files you
no longer needed. You then can delete them, move
them to another disk, or, as you will see in the next
section, archive them to preserve them for possible
future access and reduce the amount of disk space
they occupy.

```
 Path: A:\DOS\BATCH                           9-13-91  8:38:15 am
┌──────────────────────────────────────────┐ ┌──────────────────────────┐
│ 123      .BAT      51 .a..  9-11-91 11:58:88 am │ FILE  *.*               │
│ 123      .BAT      44 .a..  1-89-91  9:25:46 am │                         │
│ 123      .PIF     545 .a..  8-38-98  1:23:82 am │ DISK  A:                │
│ 123      .PIF     545 .a..  7-83-98  9:58:56 am │ Available               │
│ 123R23   .BAT      23 .a..  3-85-91 12:51:24 pm │   Bytes       211,968   │
│ 123R23   .BAT      23 .a..  3-85-91 12:51:24 pm │                         │
│ 123W     .EXE  36,592 .a..  8-15-91  1:23:88 am │ GLOBAL Statistics       │
│ 123W     .EXE  36,592 .a..  8-15-91  1:23:88 am │ Total                   │
│ 123W     .RI       96 .a..  8-15-91  1:23:88 am │   Files         1,551   │
│ 123W     .RI       96 .a..  8-15-91  1:23:88 am │   Bytes    54,461,479   │
│ 123W     .V18       1 .a..  8-15-91  1:23:88 am │ Matching                │
│ 123W     .V18       1 .a..  8-15-91  1:23:88 am │   Files         1,551   │
│ 3DAREA   .WK3   1,539 .a..  7-24-91 11:38:26 am │   Bytes    54,461,479   │
│ 3DAREA   .WK3   1,539 .a..  7-24-91 11:38:26 am │ Tagged                  │
│ 3DBAR    .WK3   1,539 .a..  7-24-91 11:18:48 am │   Files             6   │
│ 3DBAR    .WK3   1,539 .a..  7-24-91 11:18:48 am │   Bytes        48,875   │
│ @EASE6   .WK3  15,866 .a..  3-15-98  1:88:88 am │ Current File            │
│ @EASE6   .WK3  15,866 .a..  3-15-98  1:88:88 am │ 123         .BAT        │
│ ADAPTEC  .ZIP   1,898 .a..  1-38-91 12:32:24 pm │   Bytes            51   │
├──────────────────────────────────────────┴─┴──────────────────────────┤
│FILE       Attributes  Copy  Delete  Edit  Filespec  Invert  Log disk  Move  │
│COMMANDS   New date  Open  Print  Rename  Tag  Untag  View  eXecute  Quit    │
│◄─┘ tree   F7 autoview  F8 split    F9 menu  F10 commands   F1 help  ESC cancel│
└──────────────────────────────────────────────────────────────────────┘
```

Fig. 5.7. The result of the Alt+F4 compare command.

Archiving and Extracting Files

Archiving is the process of storing one or more files in a special type of file called a *library* or *archive*. You must extract files from the archive before you can use those files. When files are stored in archives, they are compressed, so they use considerably less disk space than uncompressed files.

Understanding Archiving

Estimating how much less disk space compressed files will require is difficult. Often, an estimate of 50 percent is given, but too many factors are involved for any estimate to have good accuracy. Graphics images, such as the screens in this book, for example, usually reduce much more than program files.

Another factor in determining how much space archiving files will save is the way DOS itself allocates disk space. DOS always allocates at least one cluster of space to any file. A cluster varies in size depending on the disk, but it is at least 512 bytes on a diskette, and 2048 bytes is typical on a hard disk. If you have twenty small batch files of about 20 bytes each on your hard disk, they use at least 40,960 bytes—not 400 bytes as you might expect from their reported size. If you archive all these batch files, the resulting archive file would use a single cluster—a 95 percent saving—and would still have room to store about sixty more 20-byte files!

Regardless of the actual percentage savings, archiving files you don't currently need or files you intend to transmit through a modem results in much higher efficiency.

Several different, noncompatible archiving formats
have been developed over the years. For some time,
the ARC format (named for the file extension used on
archive files) was popular. Later, the ZIP format be-
came the primary archive format, in part because it
usually resulted in greater compression percentages.
XTree uses the ZIP format, but includes a separate
program to convert ARC format archives to ZIP format archives.

 NOTE Many manufacturers use a proprietary
archiving format to compress their program files. XTree cannot extract files compressed using these formats or any of the
other proprietary formats, such as ZOO.

Archiving Files

To compress files and add them to an archive, you
must first tag the files. You can add files to a new
archive or an existing one. If the archive file you
specify does not already exist, XTree creates a new
archive using the name that you specify. If it does
already exist, XTree simply adds the new files to
those already in the archive.

Before you can create or add files to an archive, you
must first make a file window active. Then follow
these steps:

1. Tag the files to be archived. You can tag the files
   using any of XTree's file-tagging methods; select
   the one that best suits your needs.

2. Press F10 (or use the mouse) and select Zip
   from the Tagged drop-down menu. If you prefer,
   press Ctrl+F5 to activate the Zip command.

   XTree prompts you for a name for the archive
   file (see fig. 5.8).

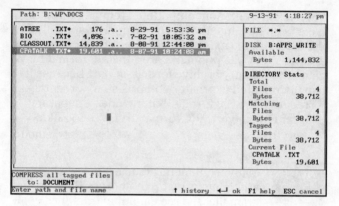

Fig. 5.8. Entering a name for the archive file.

3. Type the file name for the archive file (such as **DOCUMENT**) and press **Enter**. Do not add an extension to the name for now; XTree uses the ZIP extension by default.

   XTree presents a menu of options. You can select one of the following choices:

Option	Function
Paths	If set to yes, XTree can save the path name information along with each file. This setting enables the files to later be extracted automatically to the correct directories.
Encryption	If set to yes, XTree scrambles files as it stores them in the archive. The files can then be extracted only by someone who knows the correct password (which you must enter if you select this option). Without the password, extracting the files is impossible; use this option with caution.

Option	Function
Option	*Function*
Method (available only when adding files to an existing archive file)	Selects the method of adding files to the archive. The three methods include add (adds all tagged files to the archive), update (adds new files or replaces changed files in the archive), and freshen (replaces only changed files in the archive).
Speed/size	Toggles XTree's compression method between the fastest compression and a method that is slower but might result in a greater compression ratio.

4. Select any of the options by pressing the high-lighted letter or pointing with the mouse and clicking the left mouse button.

5. Press Enter to continue after you set the options as you want them. XTree then moves the high-light through the tagged files and adds the files to the archive.

Creating Archives in Self-Extracting Format

You also can create self-extracting archive files that don't need another program to help them extract their files. Self-extracting archive files use the ZIP format, but with two changes. First, the archive file has the extension EXE; second, the resulting archive file is somewhat larger because it includes a small program for extracting its contents.

You create self-extracting archive files in exactly the same way you create any other archives, except that you add the extension EXE when you enter the archive name.

NOTE Self-extracting archive files cannot contain a file with the same name as the archive. You cannot, for example, add a program file called DOCUMENT.EXE to a self-extracting archive that is also called DOCUMENT.EXE.

Extracting Archived Files

After you create archive files, you must first open the archive before you can extract files from it. When you open an archive, XTree displays it in a ZIP or archive window.

Suppose, for example, that you want to extract all files in the archive whose file names started with 123. To extract the files from an archive, follow these steps:

1. In a standard XTree directory window, highlight the directory that contains the archive file.

2. Press Enter to move the highlight to the small file window.

3. If necessary, highlight the archive file.

4. Press Alt+F5 to open a ZIP directory window.

   To open a ZIP or archive window, highlight a file with a ZIP or ARC extension (in a file window) and press Alt+F5. The same command opens either type of window (depending on the type of archive file).

   If the file that was highlighted when you issued the command used the default ZIP format, the window that opens is a ZIP window. If the file used the older ARC format, an archive window opens. If the highlighted file is a self-extracting archive, an error message appears to alert you that the file is an unknown file type. To continue, press Z to select Zip format.

NOTE XTreeGold 2.5 fully supports the ZIP format for archiving files. It can extract but not create ARC format archive files. To convert ARC format archives to ZIP format, you use a separate program— ARC2ZIP.EXE—that is included with XTreeGold 2.5.

5. Select the type of file window you want. Press S, for example, to select Showall. A showall ZIP file window opens that displays all files in the archive, regardless of their location in the archive.

   The ZIP window also can display a small ZIP file window, an expanded ZIP file window, a branch ZIP file window, and a showall ZIP file window. Each of these ZIP windows is similar to the corresponding standard XTree file windows, and you select them in the same way that you select the corresponding standard XTree file windows.

   If the ZIP file contains directory path information, highlight a directory in the ZIP directory window that contains files. Press Enter once for a small ZIP file window, twice for an expanded ZIP file window, and three times to return to the ZIP directory window.

   While the ZIP directory window is active, select Branch for a ZIP branch window or Showall for a ZIP showall window.

6. If you want, use the Filespec command to display different files.

7. Tag the files you want to extract.

   You can use the Tag command to tag individual files, Ctrl+Tag to tag all files in the window, or Alt+Tag to tag files using file attributes. You can use the right mouse button to toggle file tags, and you can use the drop-down Tag menu.

8. Decide whether you want to extract the files to a single directory or to their original directories.

   The Ctrl+Extract command extracts the files to a single directory (which you specify in step 10). The Alt+Extract command extracts the files to the original directories. If the original directories no longer exist, XTree creates them.

9. Specify the file names. Press Enter to extract the files using their original names. You can specify a wild card filespec if you want to change the names of the extracted files.

10. Enter the destination path, which is the name of the directory that will contain the extracted files.

11. Press Y to select Yes if you want the extracted files to automatically replace existing files with the same names. Press N to select No if you want XTree to prompt you before overwriting existing files.

12. If the archive was created using a password, type the password and press Enter. If the archive is not password-protected, just press Enter.

XTree then begins the process of extracting the tagged files. As it extracts each file, the highlight moves down the list to the file currently being extracted. When all the tagged files have been extracted, you can select additional files to extract, delete files from the archive, or exit from the ZIP window.

To delete files from an archive, tag the files you want to delete. To tag files, follow the same procedure you used to tag files for extraction. Press Ctrl+Delete to delete the tagged files. If you want to delete a single file from an archive, highlight the file and select Delete.

When you finish manipulating files in the archive file, press Esc once or twice (depending on which ZIP window is active) to return to the normal XTree display. XTree does not automatically update the file window display after you extract files to a directory, so you must press Enter once or twice to return to the directory window. The newly extracted files appear in the file window.

When you return to the normal XTree display, the Filespec command you used in the ZIP file window is canceled. XTree restores any filespec setting that was in effect before you opened the archive file.

Simply extracting files from an archive does not delete the files from the archive. If you make changes to some of the extracted files, you can update those files in the archive by selecting freshen as the method of adding files to the archive when you archive the files again. (For more information, see "Archiving Files" earlier in this chapter.)

Printing Files

XTree can print the contents of individual files or groups of tagged files, but you should only use this feature to print simple text files (which are also often called ASCII files).

You will find that the best use of XTree's printing capabilities is to provide a printed copy of batch files and the documentation files often included with programs. These documentation files often have a name similar to READ.ME, README.TXT, or README.DOC.

If your word processor program includes a documentation file with a name similar to those mentioned in the preceding paragraph, the documentation file is probably not a simple text file but is in the word processor's format. Word processor format files usually contain special codes that indicate to the word processing program which type of formatting should be applied to blocks of text. These codes can cause problems when you attempt to print the file using XTree.

As an example, suppose that you want a printed copy of each of your batch files. You keep all batch files in a subdirectory called BATCH under your DOS directory. To print these batch files, follow these steps:

1. Make sure that your printer is on and contains plenty of paper. XTree begins each file printout on a new page, so even one- or two-line batch files use an entire sheet of paper.

2. Press Enter once or twice, as necessary, to make the directory window active.

3. Highlight the directory containing the files to be printed. In this case, highlight C:\DOS\BATCH.

4. Press Enter to make the small file window active. If you prefer working in an expanded file window, press Enter again.

5. If necessary, change the filespec to limit the file display. If the directory contains files other than batch files, use the Filespec command to change the displayed filespec to *.BAT.

6. Tag the files you want to print. For the example, press Ctrl+Tag to tag all the displayed files. If you don't want to print all the batch files, either highlight them and select Untag, or use Tag (not Ctrl+Tag) to tag the desired files in the window.

7. Press F10 and select print from the Tagged menu or press Ctrl+Print.

   XTree prompts you for the number of lines to print per page. The default setting of 55 is usually correct, but you might need to adjust this number to suit your printer and the length of the paper. See your printer manual for more information on changing the form length setting.

8. If you want to use a different number of lines, type the number but do not press Enter.

   By default, XTree prints a page header at the top of each page. This page header includes the directory that contains the file being printed; the file name and extension; the size, attributes, date, and time for the file; and a page number.

9. To toggle the headers setting and control whether headers are printed, press F2.

10. Press Enter to begin printing the tagged files. To cancel printing, press Esc.

NOTE XTree issues a form-feed command to the printer after printing each file. The paper advances to the position that the printer determines is the top of the next sheet of paper. The top-of-form point is usually set when the printer is turned on, and it normally is considered to be every 11 inches. If the paper is not in the correct position when you turn on the power, XTree might begin printing in the middle of the page. To correct this problem, press Esc to tell XTree to stop printing. Then turn off the printer and adjust the paper so that printing starts at the top of a page. Turn on the printer again and reissue the command you used to print the file or files.

Viewing Files

XTree can display many files in their native format. That is, if you have a dBASE file or a Lotus 1-2-3 file, XTree can display them as they would appear if you were using dBASE or 1-2-3 to load and display the file. You also can view files before attempting to print them (see "Printing Files" earlier in this chapter) so that you can make certain they are text files and do not contain special formatting that could cause printing problems.

NOTE XTree uses file viewers to display files in their native format. These viewers are installed when you install XTree. If you did not install the viewers when you installed XTree, you can use the installation program to add them now. See Appendix A for more information on installing XTree.

XTree has two different view windows. The autoview window has a listing of files in the current directory along the left side of the screen and a partial view of the file to the right. As you scroll through the files, the right side of the screen changes to display each file. If the proper viewer has been installed and the highlighted file is not a graphics format file, the file appears in native format. If the highlighted file does not have a viewer, the file contents appear, but they are not formatted. Unformatted views of files are difficult to understand because additional characters not normally displayed might appear mixed in with text.

Using the Autoview Window

You invoke the autoview window by pressing F7 or by selecting Autoview from the drop-down Window menu (see fig. 5.9). You can switch to an autoview window whether XTree is currently displaying a directory window or a file window, and the files that appear in the current file window also appear in the autoview window.

```
Path: C:\SYMPHONY\DBF

BCTEST    .ZIP   DATE      EXPENSE   INCOME   DESCRIPT
CONTRACT.DBF     19881210    25.33            Technical Manuals
LEDGER   .DBF    19881223  1189.00            NEC Printer
                 19881230    42.39            Office furniture
                 19881230    94.76            Office furniture
                 19890101   155.82            Office furniture
                 19890103  5772.00            Computer
                 19890106   333.37            Software
                 19890109   209.85            Office furniture
                 19890114     7.95            Cable
                 19890114   137.75            Modem
                 19890117    39.88            Business cards
                 19890119    18.73            Telephone equipment
                 19890120    15.00            Software
                 19890120    25.00            Office postage
                 19890120    55.50            Software
                 19890122   127.18            Office Furniture
                 19890124    15.90            Cable
                 19890124    22.95            Subscription

AUTOVIEW   Attributes  Copy  Delete  Edit  Filespec  Invert  Move
COMMANDS   New date  Open  Print  Rename  Tag  Untag  View  eXecute
           F9 menu   F10 commands                    F1 help  ESC cancel
```

Fig. 5.9. The autoview window.

To use the autoview window, first highlight the directory containing the files you want to view. If you want to view the files displayed in a branch, showall, or global window, select the type of window.

Using the View Window

The other type of view window displays more of a file's contents. Instead of displaying a file listing along the left side of the screen as the autoview window does, the view window uses the entire width of the screen to display the file contents (see fig. 5.10).

If you own XTreeGold 2.5 or later, you also can use the view window to display several types of graphics files in their native format. XTree supplies several sample graphics images in different formats.

```
File: C:\SYMPHONY\DBF\LEDGER.DBF        Record:  1/211

DATE      EXPENSE    INCOME    DESCRIPT
19881210     25.33             Technical Manuals
19881223   1189.00             NEC Printer
19881230     42.39             Office furniture
19881230     94.76             Office furniture
19890101    155.82             Office furniture
19890103   5772.00             Computer
19890106    333.37             Software
19890109    209.85             Office furniture
19890114      7.95             Cable
19890114    137.75             Modem
19890117     39.88             Business cards
19890119     18.73             Telephone equipment
19890120     15.00             Software
19890120     25.00             Office postage
19890120     55.50             Software
19890122    127.18             Office Furniture
19890124     15.90             Cable
19890124     22.95             Subscription

VIEW        ASCII  Dump  Gather  Hex  Structure  Wordwrap
COMMANDS    F2 go to record  F9 search  SPACE search again
↑↓ scroll                              F10 commands  F1 help  ESC cancel
```

Fig. 5.10. Displaying a dBASE file in a view window.

The view window is available when XTree is displaying a file window or an autoview window. To use a
view window to display a file's contents, first highlight the file you want to view in either a file window
or an autoview window. Next select View to display
the file's contents. If the proper viewer was installed,
the file appears in native format; otherwise, the file
appears unformatted.

NOTE   If the graphics files supplied with XTree
have not already been copied to your
XTree directory, first copy the files. The
following example assumes that the graphics files are located in C:\XTGOLD.

To view COLUMBIA.DWG, one of the sample graphics
image files provided with XTree, follow these steps:

1. Highlight the XTGOLD directory in the directory
   window.

2. Press Enter once to make the small file window
   active (or twice if you prefer an expanded file
   window).

3. Highlight COLUMBIA.DWG.

4. Press **F7** to change to the autoview window. This step is optional, but it shows you the type of the graphics file.

5. Select **V**iew to view the file in AutoCAD format. XTree provides a progress report as it converts the file for viewing. Figure 5.11 shows COLUMBIA.DWG displayed in the view window.

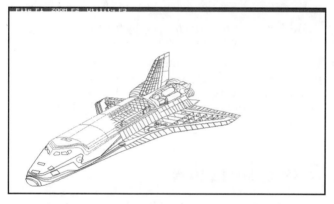

Fig. 5.11. Displaying COLUMBIA.DWG in a view window.

6. Press **Esc** to return to the autoview window.

7. Press **Esc** again to return to the file window.

If you select the view command while highlighting a file that does not have an installed viewer, XTree displays the file in one of the following formats:

- If the file is an ASCII text file, it appears in ASCII format.

- If the file contains some nontext characters, it appears in word wrap format. This format is used for most word processor files.

■ If the file contains many nontext characters, it appears in dump format. All displayable characters are shown.

You also can select other options:

Option	Function
Formatted	If the correct viewer was installed, enables you to view the file using an XTree file viewer.
Hex	Enables you to view the file as hex bytes.
Mask	Converts the view by turning off the high bit of each byte.

While you are viewing a file, XTree provides several other commands that you can use to edit files. Unless you are an experienced, advanced PC user, however, you should not attempt to edit files in the XTree view window.

Searching Files

XTree can search all tagged files for specific text strings. You can search files when any file window or an autoview window is active.

When you use the Ctrl+Search command, you start by tagging the range of files for XTree to search. After XTree completes its search, only those files containing the specified text string remain tagged. XTree does not include a search command that applies to individual untagged files; you can only search tagged files.

As an example of the search command, suppose that you want to find which of your batch files includes a command to load a mouse driver. To accomplish the search, follow these steps:

1. From a directory window, highlight the directory containing the batch files. In this case, highlight C:\DOS\BATCH.

2. Press Enter once to make a small file window active (or twice if you prefer an expanded file window).

3. Tag the files in the directory by pressing Ctrl+Tag. In this example, tag the files in the C:\DOS\BATCH directory.

4. Select Ctrl+Search. XTree prompts you for the search string.

5. Enter the text you want to find. For example, type mouse.

6. Press Enter to begin the search. XTree highlights each file in the list as it searches the files. Each file that contains the search string *mouse* remains tagged; all other files are untagged. Figure 5.12 shows the result of the search.

```
 Path: C:\DOS\BATCH                                    9-14-91  3:12:43 pm
┌─────────────────────────────────────────────────┬───────────────────────┐
│ 123     .BAT◆      44 .a..   SYM    .BAT◆     95 .a..  │FILE  *.*              │
│ 123R23  .BAT◆      23 .a..   SYMOUSE.BAT◆     13 ....  │                       │
│ 2HIGH   .    ◆      3 ....   SYMS   .BAT◆  1,068 ....  │DISK  C:Fixed C        │
│ AF      .BAT◆      14 ....   TTIME  .BAT◆     42 ....  │ Available             │
│ AFS     .BAT◆      31 ....   WINSET .BAT◆    736 .a..  │  Bytes   10,385,408   │
│ CAD     .BAT◆      33 ....                             │                       │
│ CSAM    .BAT◆      37 ....                             │DIRECTORY Stats        │
│ FORMFEED.BAT◆       2 ....                             │ Total                 │
│ IN      .BAT◆      41 .a..                             │  Files            24  │
│ INC     .BAT◆      20 ....                             │  Bytes         3,185  │
│ LET     .BAT◆      56 ....                             │ Matching              │
│ LISTARC .BAT◆     115 ....                             │  Files            24  │
│ LISTARC1.BAT◆      43 ....                             │  Bytes         3,185  │
│ LISTZIP .BAT◆     127 .a..                             │ Tagged                │
│ LISTZIP1.BAT◆      48 ....                             │  Files            24  │
│ NEW-VARS.BAT◆     180 ....                             │  Bytes         3,185  │
│ QA      .BAT◆      30 ....                             │ Current File          │
│ QC      .BAT◆     336 ....                             │  123     .BAT         │
│ SHOWARC .BAT◆      48 ....                             │  Bytes            44  │
├───────────────────────────────────────────────────────┴───────────────────────┤
│Search all tagged files for text: mouse                                          │
├────────────────────────────────────────────────────────────────────────────────┤
│Enter a search string                    ↑ history  ↵ ok  F1 help  ESC cancel    │
└────────────────────────────────────────────────────────────────────────────────┘
```

Fig. 5.12. The result of using the Ctrl+Search command.

XTree ignores the case of the letters when looking for the search string in each file.

Summary

This chapter examined XTree's more advanced file management capabilities, including specifying the sort order, comparing file lists, archiving and extracting files, printing file contents, viewing many different types of files, and searching through files for specified text strings. Chapter 6 examines managing directories.

Managing Directories

The XTree file management capabilities discussed in previous chapters only affected single files or groups of files. This chapter expands the discussion of XTree's file management capabilities by examining directory management.

A directory is actually a special type of DOS file that you use to organize and manage the other files on your disk. To manage a disk's directory structure, you use special DOS commands that apply only to directories. XTree also has some special capabilities for managing directories.

Creating Directories

The most basic directory management function is creating new directories. In creating new directories, you are building the foundation for organized file management.

NOTE

Remember that all disks automatically have a root directory that you reference by placing a backslash (\) at the beginning of a path specification. You cannot create, delete, or rename the root directory. All named directories on a disk are subdirectories below the root directory.

Before you can use XTree to create a new directory, a directory window must be the active window. If necessary, press Enter once or twice (depending on the currently active window) to make a directory window active.

Suppose that you just bought a new word processing program. You now want to create a new directory called WORD under the root directory for the program files and two subdirectories under WORD for your document files. To use XTree to create the directories, follow these steps:

1. In the active directory window, press Home or use the arrow keys to move the highlight to the root directory, or point to the root directory with the mouse and click the left mouse button.

   You might want to create a directory within another directory. If so, highlight the directory in which you want to place the new directory.

2. Select Make from either the DIR COMMANDS menu at the bottom of the screen or the drop-down Directory menu.

   XTree prompts you, as you see in figure 6.1.

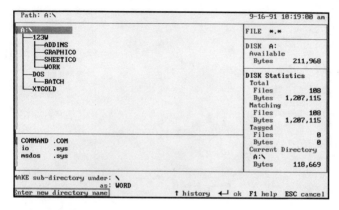

Fig. 6.1. Entering the name of the new directory.

3. Type the name of the new directory—in this case WORD—and press Enter. You cannot change the parent directory of the new directory; the directory you have highlighted appears following the prompt Make subdirectory under:. If the prompt shows a directory name other than the one you intended as the parent of the new directory, press Esc and return to step 1.

To create the additional directories, highlight the newly created directory—in this case, WORD—and select Make again. Type the name of the new directory to create under the existing directory and press Enter.

For this example, enter DOC1 and press Enter. Then Select Make again. Type DOC2 as the name of the second new directory to create under \WORD and press Enter. Your screen now looks like figure 6.2.

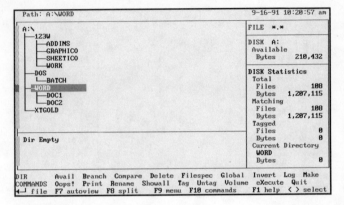

Fig. 6.2. The result of creating three new directories.

Your new directories are empty, but they are ready for you to use. In this example, you learned that you use the same method to create subdirectories under either the root directory or under subdirectories of the root directory.

Removing Directories

Removing directories often involves several considerations. One important consideration is whether to first copy (or move) the directory's files elsewhere or to delete the files in the process of removing the directory. Another possibility is simply to move the entire directory with its files and any subdirectories to another location on the same or another disk. Keep in mind that when you remove a directory, you also affect any files and subdirectories that the directory contains.

XTree has two commands that you can use to remove directories. The next two sections cover the directory Delete command and the Prune command.

Deleting a Directory

XTree's directory Delete command removes empty
directories. The directory you want to remove cannot
contain any files or subdirectories when you select
the directory Delete command. If you try to remove
the WORD directory created in the previous example
without first removing the two subdirectories, XTree
will report Error: Directory not empty. Although
the three new directories do not contain any files, the
two subdirectories under WORD cause an error con-
dition.

To remove a directory using the directory Delete
command, first remove any subdirectories and files
that the directory contains. (For information about
deleting files, see Chapter 4.)

After the subdirectory is empty, select the Delete
command from the DIR COMMANDS menu at the bottom of the screen or from the drop-down Directory
menu. Select Yes to delete the highlighted directory
or No to cancel the command.

If you still receive an error message, XTree cannot
delete the directory. Be sure that you remove read-
only, hidden, or system file attributes from the files
you are trying to delete; then try again to delete the
files before deleting the directory.

Pruning a Directory

Sometimes you know that you want to delete a
directory and its contents—both files and subdirectories. In this circumstance, you don't want to
go through all the extra steps necessary when you
use the directory Delete command.

The Prune command on the drop-down directory
menu (also available as Alt+Prune) removes an entire

branch from the directory tree. This command removes the highlighted directory, any files it contains, and any subdirectories and their files.

> **CAUTION:** Before using the **P**rune command, always verify that the highlighted directory is the directory you want to remove. The **P**rune command is permanent; you cannot use the **O**ops! command to recover files from deleted directories.

To use the **P**rune command to remove the WORD directory and its two subdirectories, follow these steps:

1. Make certain that the directory window is active and the directory you want to delete—in this case, WORD—is highlighted.

2. If the selected directory or any of its subdirectories contain read-only, hidden, or system files, select **B**ranch to change to a branch window.

3. Press **Ctrl+T**ag to tag all files; then select **Ctrl+A**ttributes. Type **-R-S-H** and press **Enter** to remove any read-only, hidden, or system file attributes. Press **Enter** to return to the directory window.

> **NOTE** If the selected directory and its subdirectories do not contain any files, you will not be able to activate a branch window, and the directory window will remain active. If so, skip step 3 in this procedure, or you will tag all files in that logged disk.

4. Select **P**rune from the drop-down directory menu or press **Alt+P**rune.

5. Type **PRUNE** (see fig. 6.3) and press **Enter** to continue.

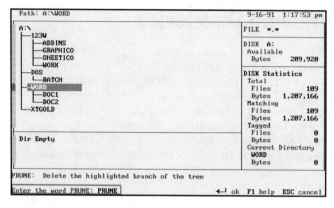

Fig. 6.3. Typing PRUNE to verify the Prune command.

XTree then deletes any files and subdirectories contained in the highlighted directory. After XTree removes the files and subdirectories, it prompts you to
specify whether you want to delete the highlighted
directory as well (see fig. 6.4). Press Yes to delete the
directory or No to keep the directory intact.

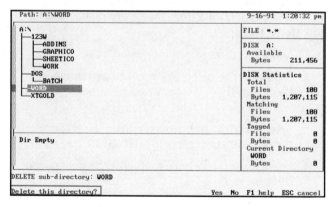

Fig. 6.4. XTree asks whether you want to remove the directory.

Moving Directories

XTree has two commands that enable you to move directories along with their files and subdirectories. One of these commands, directory menu **G**raft, is easier to use because it involves fewer steps. However, you can only use this command to move directories to another location on the same disk—along with all files in the selected directory. The file menu tagged Move with paths command is more versatile because you can specify which files should be moved, and you can specify another disk as the destination. This command requires more setup steps, however.

Using the Graft Command

The **G**raft command moves entire directories—including any files that the directories contain and any subdirectories and their files— to another location in the tree structure of the same disk.

To move a directory structure—along with all files—from one branch on a directory tree to another, follow these steps:

1. Make the directory window active.

2. Highlight the directory you want to move. All files from this directory and its subdirectories will move.

3. Select **G**raft from the drop-down Directory menu. You also can press **Alt** +**G**raft.

4. Use the arrow keys to highlight the new parent directory.

5. Press **Enter**. XTree asks you to confirm the move. Select **Y**es to continue or **N**o to cancel the move.

After you select Yes to continue, XTree moves the entire branch. In some cases, a single Alt+Graft is not possible and you have to repeat the command to make additional moves. Even so, Alt+Graft is a fast and efficient method of moving an entire directory branch elsewhere on the tree.

Using the Move with Paths Command

Although the Move with paths and Alt+Graft commands perform similar functions, several differences exist between the two commands. Move with paths is a file command and works on tagged files. Alt+Graft is a directory command and works on entire directories, whether or not they contain files. Therefore, Alt+Graft will move empty directories, but Move with paths will not. On the other hand, Move with paths can move files and their directory structures to another disk. Alt+Graft, on the other hand, can only move directories on the same disk. Also, because Move with paths works with tagged files, you can instruct it to move some files and leave other files in place.

Moving a program directory and its subdirectories from one disk to another provides a good demonstration of the Move with paths command. To move directories to another hard disk, follow these steps:

1. In the directory window, highlight the directory you want to move to the new disk.

2. Select Branch to change the window to a branch window. You then can tag all files in the current directory branch.

3. Press Ctrl+Tag to tag all files in the window. If you want to move a limited subset of the files, you also can use the Filespec command to specify the files to tag.

4. Select Move with paths from the drop-down Tagged menu. You also can press Alt+Move.

5. Press Enter to accept the original names for the files, or enter a wild card name to rename the files.

6. Specify the destination for the files. You can type the destination, press ↑ to select from the command history, or press F2 to point to the destination. Then press Enter.

   By default, XTree copies the entire path starting from the root directory. Each time you select Paths are, XTree toggles between full paths and partial branch paths.

7. Select whether to copy full paths or partial branch paths; then press Enter to continue.

8. Select Yes to have XTree replace files automatically or No to have XTree prompt you before replacing files with the same names. XTree begins moving the files.

After XTree moves the files, it returns to a directory window.

Unlike the Alt+Graft command, the Move with paths command does not remove the old directories after moving the files. If you no longer need the old directories, use the Prune command discussed earlier to remove the now-empty directory branch.

Changing Directory Names

As you organize your files on your hard disk, you might find that the original names assigned to some of your directories could be more descriptive to make them easier to remember. XTree lets you rename directories—a task DOS itself cannot perform.

> **CAUTION:** Use caution when renaming directories. Many programs require specific directory names, or they store in configuration files the names you originally assigned to their program and data directories. If you rename directories, you might need to reconfigure your programs so that they can find associated files.

A directory window must be active before you can rename a directory. Also, you must highlight the directory you want to rename before executing the Rename command. To rename a directory, follow these steps:

1. Make the directory window active and highlight the directory you want to rename.

2. Select Rename from the drop-down Directory menu or from the DIR COMMANDS menu at the bottom of the screen.

3. Type the new name for the directory.

4. Press Enter to rename the directory.

XTree renames the directory and automatically updates the directory tree to display the new directory name. Subdirectories of the renamed directory do not change, but the path to them changes. A batch file that backed up the files in the old subdirectory name, for example, would have to be changed to use the new subdirectory name instead. XTree application menus also require adjustment. (For more information about XTree application menus, see Chapter 7.)

Displaying a Directory Tree

When you start XTree, all directories on the entire disk are logged (or read), and the entire directory tree for the current disk appears in the directory window. All directories and their subdirectories appear.

XTree also enables you to log additional disk drives so that you can work with those disks, as well. Finally, XTree lets you modify the directory tree display by expanding and collapsing branches. The following sections show you how to log additional disk drives and to modify the directory tree display.

Logging Disks

XTree automatically logs the current disk when you start XTree. If you want to work with files on a different drive, you must first tell XTree to log the new drive. If you are working with diskettes, XTree also must relog the disk whenever you change diskettes. When you finish working with a disk, you can save memory by instructing XTree to release the disk.

You can log disks when either the directory window or a file window is active. In both cases, the same commands for logging disks are on the drop-down Volume menu and on the menus that appear at the bottom of the screen. Figure 6.5 shows the drop-down Volume menu with the **L**og disk option highlighted.

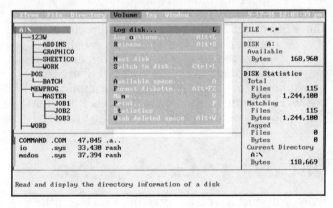

Fig. 6.5. The Log disk command highlighted on the drop-down Volume menu.

When you select **L**og disk, XTree shows which drives
are currently logged and the logging method it will
use if you log a new drive (see figure 6.6).

To select a drive for logging or to relog, type the letter of the drive or point to the drive letter at the
lower left portion of the screen and click the left
mouse button. You also can press **F2** to change the
logging method. The three options are

Option	Purpose
Full disk	All directories and files on the disk are logged.
Root only	All directories but only root directory files on the disk are logged.
Tree only	All directories but no files on the disk are logged.

Fig. 6.6. Selecting drives to log.

In most cases, you should use the full disk logging
option. This option gives you access to all files and
the directory structure. You can use the tree only
option and the root only option when you intend to
use the disk being logged as a destination disk for
operations involving disk copies. As you press **F2**,
XTree cycles through each of the options.

If you select the Log options command (or press Alt+Log), XTree enables you to select from the following options:

Option	Purpose
Branch option (also *)	Logs the current directory branch.
Disk option	Logs the entire disk.
One level option (also +)	Logs the first level of directories and files under the current directory.
Refresh	Relogs the files in the current directory.
Tree	Logs only the tree structure and releases (unlogs) all files.
Release (also Alt+Release or –)	Unlogs the Branch, the Disk drive, or all Files in branch. Because XTree keeps all logged information in memory, you might need to release a disk or branch to free memory when you need to log additional files. XTree informs you if it is out of memory.

Expanding and Collapsing the Tree

Figure 6.7 shows XTree's default tree display. All levels of all branches appear, and because there are too many directories to display on a single screen, some branches do not appear on the first screen. To view the rest of the directories, you must scroll the display using the cursor movement keys or the mouse.

```
Path: A:\                                  9-17-91 12:34:26 pm
A:\                                     FILE  *.*
 ├─123W
 │  ├─ADDINS                             DISK  A:
 │  ├─GRAPHICO                            Available
 │  ├─SHEETICO                              Bytes        168,960
 │  └─WORK
 ├─DOS                                   DISK Statistics
 │  └─BATCH                               Total
 ├─NEWPROG                                  Files            115
 │  └─MASTER                                Bytes      1,244,100
 │     ├─JOB1                             Matching
 │     ├─JOB2                               Files            115
 │     └─JOB3                               Bytes      1,244,100
 └─WORD                                   Tagged
                                            Files              0
 COMMAND .COM    47,845 .a...              Bytes              0
 io      .sys    33,430 rash            Current Directory
 msdos   .sys    37,394 rash              A:\
                                            Bytes        118,669

DIR        Avail  Branch  Compare  Delete  Filespec  Global  Invert  Log  Make
COMMANDS   Oops↑  Print   Rename   Showall  Tag  Untag  Volume  eXecute  Quit
 ↵ file    F7 autoview   F8 split    F9 menu  F10 commands    F1 help  < > select
```

Fig. 6.7. The XTree default tree display.

You can collapse and expand the directory tree
display in two ways. As discussed in the previous
section, the $+$, $*$, and $-$ keys change the display by
changing which directories and files are logged. In
addition, the F5 and F6 keys change which portions
of the tree appear on-screen without affecting
whether directories and files are logged.

The F5 key is a toggle that expands or collapses the
directory tree display to one level below the current
level. Figure 6.8 shows the effect of pressing F5 when
the highlight is on the root directory.

```
Path: A:\                                  9-17-91 12:47:10 pm
A:\                                     FILE  *.*
 · ├─123W
 · ├─DOS                                 DISK  A:
 · ├─NEWPROG                              Available
 · ├─WORD                                   Bytes        168,960
 · └─XTGOLD
                                         DISK Statistics
                                          Total
                                            Files            115
                                            Bytes      1,244,100
                                          Matching
                                            Files            115
                                            Bytes      1,244,100
                                          Tagged
                                            Files              0
 COMMAND .COM    47,845 .a...              Bytes              0
 io      .sys    33,430 rash            Current Directory
 msdos   .sys    37,394 rash              A:\
                                            Bytes        118,669

DIR        Avail  Branch  Compare  Delete  Filespec  Global  Invert  Log  Make
COMMANDS   Oops↑  Print   Rename   Showall  Tag  Untag  Volume  eXecute  Quit
 ↵ file    F7 autoview   F8 split    F9 menu  F10 commands    F1 help  < > select
```

Fig. 6.8. The effect of pressing F5 when the root directory is highlighted.

The **F6** key is also a toggle, but it expands or con-
tracts the tree to the current level. Pressing **F6**
when the root directory is highlighted collapses the
display, and none of the directories below the root
directory appear.

Collapsing and expanding the directory tree might
help when you need to manipulate files in directories
that are located far apart from each other on the tree.
If you find yourself collapsing and expanding the directory tree often, however, you may want to consider using a split window display (see Chapter 3).

Printing a Directory Listing

With XTree, you can print three different types of
directory listings. You can print the tree structure as
XTree displays it in the directory window, a listing of
the complete path names to each directory, or a listing of the files by directory.

Regardless of the type of directory listing printout,
you must have a directory window active before you
can select the command to print. Also, because the
listing of files by directory only shows tagged files,
you also must tag the files first. To print a directory
listing, follow these steps:

1. If you intend to print a listing of files by directory, use one of the methods you learned earlier
   to tag the files.

2. With the directory window active, select **P**rint
   from the drop-down Volume menu or the DIR
   COMMANDS menu. A menu appears showing the
   three directory listing options (see fig. 6.9).

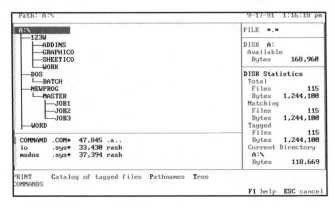

Fig. 6.9. Selecting a directory listing.

3. Select one of the following options:

Option	Purpose
Catalog of tagged files	Prints a listing by directory of all tagged files on the disk.
Pathnames	Prints the full path names to each directory.
Tree	Prints the directory tree as displayed in the XTree directory window.

4. Press **Enter** to accept the default printing of 55 lines per page. If you want a different number of lines, enter that number and press **Enter**.

XTree begins printing your selection. If necessary, you can press **Esc** to stop the printing. (Pressing **Esc**, however, will not stop the printer from printing information that is already sent.)

Adding a Volume Label

A volume label is the name you assign to a disk. It appears in the DISK box on the XTree screen and at the top of a DOS directory listing. Volume labels can help you organize your disks, especially if you print listings of the files on your disks. If you attach an adhesive label to diskettes and write the volume label on the adhesive label, you can easily match the printed listings with the diskettes.

To apply a volume label to a disk, follow these steps:

1. Make a directory window active.

2. Select Name from the drop-down Volume menu or Volume from the DIR COMMANDS menu.

   The current volume label (if any) appears, and XTree prompts you for the new name.

3. Type the new name. For this example, type XT SAMPLE (see fig. 6.10).

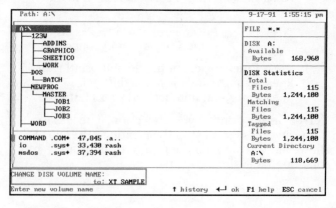

Fig. 6.10. Changing the name of a disk.

4. Press Enter to apply the new name to the disk. This name appears in the DISK box whenever the named disk is the current disk.

Disk labels can contain up to 11 characters, but cannot be the same name as a file name in the root directory or the name of a subdirectory in the root directory.

Formatting a Disk

Disks must be formatted before you can use them. Formatting is the process of placing electronic marks on the disk so that your PC knows where it can store information. New disks generally are unformatted, although some manufacturers supply formatted disks at a slightly higher cost.

XTree makes formatting disks easy because you select the drive and disk capacity from menus instead of typing a cryptic DOS command. The following example shows how to format a 360K diskette in a high capacity, 5 1/4-inch drive. You can format a diskette regardless of whether a directory window or a file window is active. Follow these steps:

1. Select **F**ormat diskette from the drop-down Volume menu (or press **Alt+F2**).

2. Type **A** to format a diskette in drive A, or **B** to format a diskette in drive B. XTree then displays the options shown in figure 6.11. (If you are formatting a 3 1/2-inch diskette, the disk capacities are 1.4m for **H**igh density and 720k for **D**ouble density.)

3. Select the correct option by pressing **H** to format a high density diskette or **D** to format a double density diskette.

```
Path: A:\                                          9-17-91  2:20:24 pm
┌─────────────────────────────────┬──────────────────────────────┐
│ A:\                             █│ FILE  *.*                    │
│  ├─123W                          │                              │
│  │  ├─ADDINS                     │ DISK  A:XT SAMPLE            │
│  │  ├─GRAPHICO                   │ Available                    │
│  │  ├─SHEETICO                   │   Bytes          168,960     │
│  │  └─WORK                       │                              │
│  ├─DOS                           │ DISK Statistics             │
│  │  └─BATCH                      │ Total                        │
│  ├─NEWPROG                       │   Files             115      │
│  │  └─MASTER                     │   Bytes       1,244,100      │
│  │     ├─JOB1                    │ Matching                     │
│  │     ├─JOB2                    │   Files             115      │
│  │     └─JOB3                    │   Bytes       1,244,100      │
│  └─WORD                          │ Tagged                       │
│                                  │   Files             115      │
├──────────────────────────────────│   Bytes       1,244,100      │
│ COMMAND .COM♦  47,845 .a..       │ Current Directory            │
│ io      .sys♦  33,430 rash       │   A:\                        │
│ msdos   .sys♦  37,394 rash       │   Bytes          118,669     │
└──────────────────────────────────┴──────────────────────────────┘
FORMAT: B
   as: 1.2m High density  360k Double density
Select media type                                  F1 help  ESC cancel
```

Fig. 6.11. Selecting disk density.

4. Press **Enter** to begin formatting. XTree reports the progress of the format. When the format is complete, XTree shows you the available space on the diskette and asks whether you want to format another diskette.

5. Press **Enter** to begin formatting another diskette or **Esc** to return to the XTree screen.

Summary

This chapter discussed XTree's directory management capabilities. You learned to use XTree to create and remove directories, move directories from one location on a directory tree to another and from one disk to another, change directory names, display portions of a directory tree, print several types of directory listings, change the name assigned to a disk, and format a diskette. These valuable skills help you manage both your directories and your files more efficiently.

In Chapter 7, you will learn to create, modify, and use XTree application menus.

Managing Application Menus

Although XTree is a powerful directory and file manager, for many XTree owners its most important function is that of an application manager or "shell" program. This chapter examines XTree's application menus and explains how to create, modify, and use them. Whether you simply want to use XTree to make your own PC easier to use, or if you are responsible for helping other XTree users set up menus of applications, this chapter contains the information you need.

It is recommended, although not mandatory, that you permit XTree to build an application menu automatically during installation. Although this chapter shows you how to create your own application menu, the menu that XTree builds automatically can serve as a model for your menus and might eliminate much of the menu-building work if you only need to make minor modifications. (See Appendix A for information on installation.)

Creating XTree Application Menus

Figure 7.1 shows a typical XTree application menu that XTree built automatically during installation. The menu lists many application programs, which are separated into several groups, such as BUSINESS, DOS UTILITIES, PROGRAMMING, and so on. If you permitted the XTree installation program to generate an application menu automatically, you already have a menu similar to this one. To display the application menu when XTree is displaying a directory or file window, press **F9**.

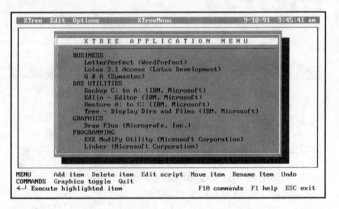

Fig. 7.1. A typical application menu that XTree generated automatically.

The text in this chapter, however, assumes that you did not ask XTree to generate an application menu automatically. Instead, the chapter explains the process of creating, using, and modifying an application menu manually. The same procedures work in either case, but by starting from scratch, you will have a better understanding of how you can create the exact menu that you want.

Understanding XTree Application Menus

Using the XTree application menu screen is similar to using the XTree directory or file windows. The words XTree, Edit, and Options appear at the top of each screen. These words are the titles of three drop-down menus. To open a menu, press F10 or move the mouse pointer to the top line and click the left mouse button.

Several menu choices—each with a highlighted letter—appear at the bottom of the screen. You can select these commands by pressing the highlighted letter or by moving the mouse pointer to the command and clicking the left mouse button. If you hold down the Alt key, additional menu selections replace those at the bottom of the screen. Pointing with the mouse to the word COMMANDS and clicking the left button once is the same as holding down the Alt key. Clicking a second time returns you to the standard menu. The same command functions exist on both the drop-down and screen menus.

The center portion of the screen is the application menu. Items on the application menu are either description lines, such as the first line and the group headings like BUSINESS, or they execute DOS commands. For example, the line that reads Lotus 3.1 Access (Lotus Development) executes the series of commands necessary to start Lotus 1-2-3. If you highlight a line with the cursor-movement keys and press Enter, or if you move the mouse pointer to the line and double-click the left mouse button, the set of commands associated with that line execute. If no commands are associated with the line, nothing happens.

Creating Your Own Application Menu

If you did not request that XTree's installation program generate an application menu automatically, you can create your own. Press **F9**; an empty XTree application menu screen appears.

> **NOTE** XTree stores its application menu in a file named XTG_MENU.DAT in the XTree program directory. If you use the file window **R**ename command to rename this file, perhaps as XTG_MENU.OLD, you can start with an empty application menu. XTree generates a new XTG_MENU.DAT file when you use the following examples. To return to the original XTree application menu, use the file window **R**ename command to rename the new XTG_MENU.DAT file as XTG_MENU.BAK; rename XTG_MENU.OLD as XTG_MENU.DAT.

Adding a Title

To begin, create a title for your menu. Follow these steps:

1. Press **A** to select **A**dd item. You also can point to **A**dd item and click the left mouse button.

2. Press the **space bar** (as many times as required to center the new title) and type the title for the menu. For example, type **Que's Custom XTree Application Menu** and press **Enter**. Your screen now looks like figure 7.2.

Adding Lines

Add a solid line below the title. Follow these steps:

1. Select Add item.

2. Hold down the **Alt** key and press **196** on the numeric keypad at the right side of your keyboard. (Do not use the keys at the top of the keyboard.) Release the **Alt** key.

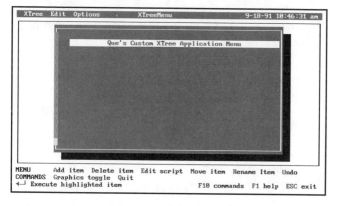

Fig. 7.2. Adding a title to the new application menu.

Repeat this step 52 more times (XTree beeps after you enter the 53rd character).

3. Press **Enter** to complete the entry (which is a single horizontal line).

4. When you select **A**dd item, XTree automatically indents the new item to match the item that was highlighted when you selected the command. Because you want to create an unindented line below the title line, select **M**ove item. Press ← to move the item one position to the left.

5. Press **Enter** to complete the entry.

Entering additional lines to your custom application menu is just as straightforward. Simply select Add item, make your entry, press Enter, and move the line, if necessary.

Adding Program Groups

Each program group can hold many program items, but you should limit the items in each group to related programs. Organizing your program groups in this manner makes your custom application menu easier to understand and use.

To add two program groups to your menu—one for business programs and one for games, for example—follow these steps:

1. Make sure that the highlight is still on the line below the title line. Use ↑ or ↓ to move the highlight, if necessary.

2. Select Add item.

3. Type the name of the group you want to add—Business, for example—and press Enter.

4. Select Move item, press →, and press Enter.

5. Select Add item.

6. Type the next program group you want to add (Games) and press Enter.

7. Select Move item, press →, and press Enter.

Your screen should now look like figure 7.3.

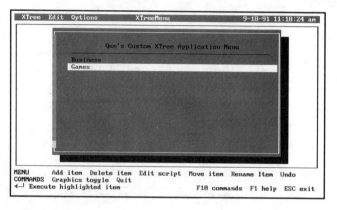

Fig. 7.3. The custom application menu with two program groups.

Adding Programs

Your application menu now has two program groups, but it does not contain any programs or any executable lines. Regardless of which line is highlighted, pressing Enter has no effect because you haven't added any commands.

The following steps show you how to add a line to the Business program group that runs Lotus 1-2-3. For this example, assume that your 1-2-3 program directory is C:\123. Follow this same procedure to add any program. Follow these steps:

1. Highlight the line that reads Business, which is the heading line for this program group.

2. Select Add item.

3. Type Lotus 1-2-3 and press Enter.

4. Select Edit script. A window appears that you use to add or edit the commands associated with an application menu item. You can enter up to 17 lines of batch file commands—the same commands you would type at the DOS prompt to execute the program.

5. Select **E**dit. The cursor moves to the beginning of line 1.

6. Type **C:**. Typing this DOS command ensures that drive C is the current drive. Then press ↓.

7. Type **CD \123**. Typing this DOS command makes \123 the current directory. Then press ↓.

8. Type **123** (the DOS command to run 1-2-3) and press **Enter**. Your screen now looks like figure 7.4.

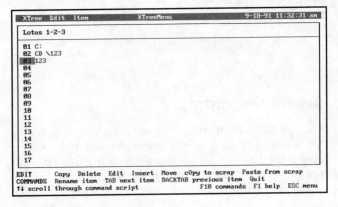

Fig. 7.4. The completed script.

9. Press **Esc** to return to the application menu.

If you highlight the program item named Lotus 1-2-3 and press **Enter**, the XTree application menu disappears and 1-2-3 executes. When you exit 1-2-3, the message Strike any key appears. Press any key to return to the XTree application menu.

If you received any error messages and 1-2-3 did not execute, your script contains an error that you must correct. To correct an error, highlight the program item, select **E**dit script, and select **E**dit. To edit an existing script, follow the same steps for adding a new script.

Next, you want to add an item under the Games program group. In this instance, however, you can permit XTree to do a little more of the work for you. In this case, the program you want to add is VPOKER.EXE, which is located in the C:\DOWNLOAD directory. To add the item, follow these steps:

1. Press Esc twice to return from the application menu screen to a directory window.

2. In the directory window, highlight the directory containing the program you want to add. In this case, highlight DOWNLOAD.

3. Press Enter to make the small file window active. (Press Enter again if you prefer an expanded file window.)

4. Highlight the program you want to add. In this case, highlight VPOKER.EXE.

5. Press F9 to return to the application menu screen.

6. Highlight the Games program group.

7. Select Add item.

8. Enter the name of the new program item, Video Poker, and press Enter.

9. Select Edit script.

10. Press F2. XTree automatically enters the three lines shown in figure 7.5. XTree uses these lines to execute the program that is currently highlighted in the file window. This shortcut method for entering the script ensures that the correct commands are entered, and it eliminates the possibility of making a typing error in the script.

```
                        XTreeMenu              9-18-91 12:02:59 pm

  Video Poker

  01 C:
  02 CD \DOWNLOAD
  03 VPOKER.EXE
  04
  05
  06
  07
  08
  09
  10
  11
  12
  13
  14
  15
  16
  17

  EDIT the DOS batch file lines

  ↑↓ scroll                                        ←┘ ok  ESC cancel
```

Fig. 7.5. XTree automatically enters three lines of text.

11. Press **Enter** to complete the script.

12. Press **Esc** to return to the application menu screen.

Highlighting the Video Poker program item and pressing **Enter**—as with the Lotus 1-2-3 program item—runs the associated script that executes the VPOKER.EXE program.

Expanding and Collapsing the Menus

Often, an XTree application menu can grow too large with too many applications. As a result, finding the program you need can be confusing because the menu might include several pages of program groups and program items.

Fortunately, XTree provides a way to collapse and expand the menu so that you can show only the program groups, expand or collapse a specified program group, or return to the original display showing all program items. The drop-down Options menu includes the following selections that expand and collapse the menu tree display:

- Expand 1 level (use + as a shortcut)

- Expand branch (use * as a shortcut)

- Collapse branch (use – as a shortcut)

When you collapse a branch on the menu, no selections appear that are indented further. If you expand one level, the selections that are indented to the first level to the right of the highlighted level appear. Expanding a branch displays all selections in the branch, regardless of how far they are indented. Figure 7.6 shows the result of highlighting the title line of the menu displayed in figure 7.1, pressing – to collapse the display so that no additional levels appear, and pressing + to display a single level—the program groups.

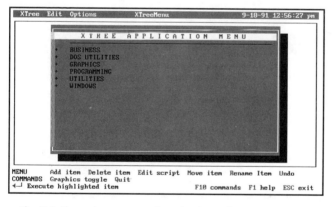

Fig. 7.6. The application menu collapsed to show only program groups.

With the application menu collapsed as in figure 7.6, finding and selecting the WINDOWS program group is easy.

Mouse users, in fact, can simply point to the space to the left of a menu item (but to the right of the scroll bar) and double-click the left mouse button to alternate between expanding and collapsing the branch.

XTree remembers which application menu branches were expanded and collapsed between sessions. The next time you start XTree, the application menu is arranged as it was when you last exited the program.

Modifying XTree Application Menus

In this section, you will learn how to delete items, rename items, and move items to another program group. You also will learn how to edit scripts so that they use XTree's special set of parameters to pass information to programs.

Deleting Items

Deleting either a program item or a program group is simple. Highlight the item you want to delete, select Delete item, and select Yes to delete the item or No to cancel the command.

When you delete an item from the XTree application menu, any items below it on the same branch are also deleted.

> **CAUTION:** Be careful when selecting menu items for deletion. If you delete an item in error, you can only add the item back by entering it manually. You would also have to redo any script that was formerly associated with deleted program items.

Renaming Items

You might want to rename XTree application menu items for several reasons. The most common is that the installation program simply makes mistakes when generating menus. Although the installation program has a large database of application programs, it is not always possible to tell from the file name which program it has found.

If you create a custom XTree application menu, you also might decide to rename items. Your employer might not appreciate seeing a Games program group on your office PC, and you might, therefore, decide that "Digital Dexterity Enhancement Applications" would be a better choice.

You can rename any item that appears on an applications menu. XTree uses the term *rename* to include any change you make to the wording of an item. Even changing *BUSINESS* to *Business* is considered renaming the item.

To rename an item on the XTree application menu, follow these steps:

1. Highlight the item you want to rename.

2. Select **R**ename Item.

3. Edit the existing entry.

   Use the **Backspace** key to remove characters, ←
   and → to move the cursor, and the **Ins** key to
   toggle between insert and overwrite mode. (In
   insert mode, the cursor is a block; in overwrite
   mode, the cursor is an underline.) Type any new
   characters needed.

4. Press **Enter** to complete the changes or **Esc** to abandon any changes.

Renaming items on the XTree applications menu has no effect on the scripts associated with program items. If you change the program item Video Poker to Monthly Sales Report, highlight **Monthly Sales Report** and press **Enter**. VPOKER.EXE will execute.

Moving Items

As you use XTree's application menu, you might find some program items that are in the wrong program group or find program groups that are arranged inefficiently. Program groups that contain the programs you most often use are easier to access if they're at the top of the menu, for example. You also can move program items to the same level as program groups if you want them to appear even when the menu is collapsed to the program group level.

Items on the application menu cannot move past an item at a higher level. First, you must change the item's status so that it is at the same level as the item you want to move it past. For example, in figure 7.1, you can move program item Backup C: to A: within the DOS UTILITIES program group, but you cannot move it directly to the BUSINESS program group. First, you must make it the same level as DOS UTILITIES; then you can move it into the BUSINESS program group. The following steps show you how to make this move. Follow this same procedure to make any move.

1. Highlight the item to move and press **M** to select **M**ove item.

2. Press ← to move the item Backup C: to A: to the same level as the program groups. (You must use the arrow keys to move application menu items; you cannot use the mouse.)

3. Press ↑ to move the item above the DOS UTILITIES program group.

4. Press → to move the item into the BUSINESS program group.

Any script associated with a program item automatically moves with the item.

Using Special Parameters in Scripts

XTree has a set of five different parameters that you can use to pass information to programs when you select an application menu item and execute a script. These parameters are

Parameter	Definition
%1	The full path name of the currently highlighted file or directory, depending on whether a file or directory window was active when the application menu was activated. For example, C:\XTGOLD\ARC2ZIP.EXE.
%2	The disk identifier of the currently highlighted file or directory. For example, C.
%3	The path name of the currently highlighted file or directory. For example, \XTGOLD.
%4	The file name of the currently highlighted file. For example, ARC2ZIP.
%5	The extension of the currently highlighted file. For example, EXE.

 NOTE XTree's special parameters are not the same as the parameters used with DOS batch programs.

Some application programs accept a file name as a command line argument. They then load that file instead of requiring you to specify the file to load after the program itself loads.

If you use a program that accepts command line arguments specifying the name of the work file, you can edit the script that loads the program so that it includes the appropriate XTree special parameter.

Suppose, for example, that the script for your word processor included these three lines:

```
C:
CD \WORD
WORD
```

You could edit the script to read

```
C:
CD \WORD
WORD %4
```

Now the file name that was highlighted in the file window when the application menu was activated is used as a command line argument.

Use the following steps to edit the script associated with the word processing program item; follow the same basic steps to edit any script.

1. Highlight the program item line for the word processing program.

2. Select Edit script.

3. Move the cursor to line 3.

4. Select Edit.

5. Move the cursor to the end of the line and type %4.

6. Press Enter.

7. Press Esc to return to the application menu.

To use the modified application menu item, press Esc twice to return to the directory window. Highlight the directory that contains your document files and press

Enter to move to the file window. Highlight the document file you want to load with your word processor. Press F9 to return to the application menu. Highlight the word processor program item and press Enter.

This example assumes that your word processor has been configured so that it already knows which directory contains your document files. You can modify the example to provide the complete path name of the document file to the word processor by substituting %1 for %4. Be sure, however, that you always use care to make certain that a document file is highlighted in a file window before you select the word processor program item and press Enter. Otherwise, your word processor might attempt to load a highlighted file that is not a document file. If so, the results could be unpredictable.

Modifying Configuration Settings

Two items of XTree's configuration settings directly apply to the application menus. The first determines whether the application menu or the directory window is the default active window when XTree is loaded. The second determines whether you can modify the application menu.

To make the following changes to XTree's configuration, a file window must be active and the XTree program directory must be the current directory. If the application menu window is active, press Esc twice to return to a directory window. Highlight the XTree program directory and press Enter. Highlight XTG_CFG.EXE. Next, select eXecute. Press Enter at the prompt to run XTree's configuration program. XTree displays the Configuration main menu (see fig. 7.7).

NOTE

Do not attempt to use Alt+F10 or the Configuration option on the drop-down XTree menu to change these configuration items. If you use one of these options to access the Configuration menu, you can change whether the application menu or the directory window is the default active window whenever XTree is loaded. You cannot, however, change the setting that controls whether you can modify the application menu.

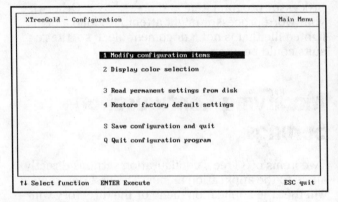

Fig. 7.7. The Configuration main menu.

Select 1 Modify configuration items. XTree displays the first page of configuration items that you can modify (see fig. 7.8). To make the application menu display automatically, select 1 Opening screen is the Application Menu and change the setting from NO to YES.

```
XTreeGold - Configuration Items                              Page 1
Application Menu
    1 Opening screen is the Application Menu          NO
    2 Pause after application program execution       YES

Directories
    3 Program path:                                   C:\XTGOLD
    4 Editor program:

Disk logging
    5 Disk logging method                             QUICK
    6 Log disk commands only read the root directory  NO
    7 Log disk commands only read the directory tree  NO




  Next page    Main menu
Show the next screen of configuration items.
↑↓ Select item   ENTER Change item            ESC Return to main menu
```

Fig. 7.8. Page 1 of the configuration items.

Next, to disallow changes to the application menu, select Next page four times until page 5 appears.

Select 1 Allow modifications to Application Menu to toggle between settings. If you select NO for this setting, you cannot modify the menu (until you change the setting back to YES).

Select Main menu to return to the Configuration main menu (refer back to fig. 7.7). To save your changes and return to XTree, select S Save configuration and quit. Press Enter to save the configuration. Press Esc to return to XTree.

Summary

This chapter examined XTree's application menus and how to create, modify, and use them. The chapter included creating, using, and modifying XTree application menus, as well as modifying XTree's application menu-related configuration settings.

Chapter 8 is a reference of all the commands in XTreeGold and XTree Easy.

Command Reference

This chapter provides a command reference to XTreeGold and XTree Easy. This reference is task-oriented so that you easily can find the commands you need.

XTreeGold includes all the commands listed. Where XTree Easy does not include a command function, the listing indicates "Not included in XTree Easy."

Application Menu

Purpose

Displays the XTree application menu, which enables you to select programs from your hard disk. You can change the menu by adding items, changing their actions, or controlling how much of the menu appears.

To display the menu

Press F9 while any directory or file window is active.

To change the menu

Select one of the following options:

Option	Function
Add item	Adds a position for a new item.
Delete items	Deletes a specified item from the application menu.
Edit script	Edits the command script associated with the highlighted item.
Move item	Moves a highlighted item to another position on the application menu.
Rename item	Changes the text of a highlighted item.
Undo changes	Removes editing changes.
Graphics toggle	Toggles between displaying and not displaying branch lines.
Expand 1 level (or +)	Expands the current branch to one level beyond the highlighted level.
Expand branch (or *)	Completely expands the current branch.
Collapse branch (or −)	Collapses the current branch.

Attributes

Purpose

Modifies the file attributes of a single file or a group of tagged files.

To change the attributes of a single file

1. In the directory window, highlight the directory containing the file.

2. Press Enter to make the file window active.

3. Highlight the file.

4. From the drop-down File menu or the FILE COMMANDS menu, select Attributes.

5. Specify the attributes to change:

   +R makes the file read-only.

   -R removes the read-only attribute.

   +A sets the archive attribute on.

   -A sets the archive attribute off.

   +S adds the system attribute.

   -S removes the system attribute.

   +H adds the hidden attribute.

   -H removes the hidden attribute.

   Do not leave any spaces between the attributes.

6. Press Enter to make the attribute changes.

To change the attributes of a group of tagged files

1. In the directory window, highlight the directory containing the files.

2. Press Enter to make the file window active.

3. Tag the files you want to change.

4. From the drop-down Tagged menu, select Attributes. You also can select Ctrl+Attributes from the CTRL FILE COMMANDS menu.

5. Specify the attributes to change. (See step 5 of the preceding procedure.) Do not leave any spaces between the attributes.

6. Press Enter to make the attribute changes.

Autoview

Purpose

Displays file contents.

Not included in XTree Easy

To display file contents

1. Select the directory containing the files to view.

2. From the drop-down Window menu or the DIR COMMANDS or FILE COMMANDS menu, select Autoview.

3. Move the highlight up or down through the list of files to view the desired files.

Available Space

Purpose

Displays available space on a specified disk.

To display available space

1. From the drop-down Volume menu or the DIR COMMANDS menu, select Available.

2. Select the disk to display.

3. Press Enter to return to the menu.

Batch

Purpose

Executes a DOS batch file using the tagged files.

Not included in XTree Easy

To execute a batch file

1. In the directory window, highlight the directory containing the files and press Enter to make the file window active.

2. Tag the files you want to use with the batch file.

3. From the drop-down Tagged menu, select Batch. You also can select Ctrl+Batch from the CTRL FILE COMMANDS menu.

4. Type the batch file command line—up to 127 characters.

5. Press Enter to execute the command line.

Branch

Purpose

Changes the active window to a branch file window. This window displays all files in a directory branch.

Not included in XTree Easy

To change the active window to a branch file window

1. In the directory window, highlight the parent directory of the branch you want to display in the branch file window.

2. From the DIR COMMANDS menu, press B to select Branch. You also can select Branch files from the drop-down Window menu.

Compare

Purpose

Compares directory listings in different directories. Finds duplicate or unique file names.

Not included in XTree Easy

To compare two specified directories

1. In the directory window, highlight the directory that contains the first group of files.

2. From the Directory drop-down menu, select Compare.

3. Select the second directory.

4. Select the compare options:

Option	Function
Identical	Lists files with the same name and date.
Unique	Lists files that do not exist in the second directory.
Newer	Lists files in the first directory that have a more recent date than identically named files in the second directory.
Older	Lists files in the first directory that have an older date than identically named files in the second directory.

5. Press Enter to tag files meeting the selected criteria.

To compare files across all directories or disks

1. Make a branch, showall, or global file window active, depending on whether you want to compare all files in the branch, on the disk, or on all disks.

2. Select Alt+Compare.

3. Select Scope (global window only).

4. Select the compare options:

Option	Function
Duplicate name	Lists files with duplicate names, regardless of dates.

Option	Function
Unique names	Lists files with unique names.
Identical dates	Lists files with duplicate names and the same date.
Newest date	Lists the newest version of files with duplicate names.
Oldest date	Lists the oldest version of files with duplicate names.

Configuration

Purpose

Accesses the XTree configuration program.

To make configuration changes

1. From the drop-down XTree menu, select **C**onfiguration. You also can press **Alt +F10** from the ALT DIR COMMANDS or ALT FILE COMMANDS menu.

2. Select the configuration item to change.

3. Press **Esc** one or more times to return to XTree.

Copy File

Purpose

Copies single files or a group of tagged files. Optionally, it can copy directory structures with files.

To copy a single file

1. In the directory window, highlight the directory containing the file and press Enter to make the file window active.

2. Highlight the file to copy.

3. From the drop-down File menu or the FILE COMMANDS menu, select Copy.

4. Type a new name for the file and press Enter. To copy the file without changing its name, simply press Enter.

5. Type the name of the destination directory. You also can press F2 to enter point mode and select the destination directory.

6. Press Enter to copy the file.

To copy a group of tagged files

1. In the directory window, highlight the directory containing the files and press Enter to make the file window active.

2. Tag the files you want to copy.

3. From the drop-down Tagged menu, select Copy. You also can select Ctrl+Copy from the CTRL FILE COMMANDS menu.

4. Type a new wild card name for the files and press Enter. To copy the files without changing their names, simply press Enter.

5. Type the name of the destination directory. You also can press F2 to enter point mode and select the destination directory.

6. Select Yes to overwrite existing files automatically. Select No to be prompted before existing files are overwritten.

7. Press Enter to copy the files.

To copy a group of tagged files along with their directory structures

1. In the directory window, highlight the directory containing the files and press Enter to make the file window active.

2. Tag the files you want to copy.

3. From the drop-down Tagged menu, select Copy with paths. You also can select Alt+Copy from the ALT FILE COMMANDS menu.

4. Type a new wild card name for the files and press Enter. To copy the files without changing their names, simply press Enter.

5. Type the name of the destination directory. You also can press F2 to enter point mode and select the destination directory.

6. Select Yes to overwrite existing files automatically. Select No to be prompted before existing files are overwritten.

7. Press Enter to copy the files.

Delete Directory

Purpose

Removes a single directory or a directory branch.

Not included in XTree Easy

To remove a single directory

1. In the directory window, highlight the directory that you want to delete.

2. Make a file window active and delete all files in the directory.

3. Press Esc to return to the directory window.

4. From the drop-down Directory menu, select Delete.

5. Select Yes to delete the directory or No to cancel the deletion.

To remove a directory branch

1. In the directory window, highlight highest level directory in branch to be deleted.

2. From the drop-down Directory menu, select Prune. You also can select Alt+Prune from the ALT DIR COMMANDS menu.

3. Type PRUNE and press Enter.

4. Select Yes to delete the directory branch or No to cancel the deletion.

Delete File

Purpose

Deletes a selected file or group of tagged files.

To delete a single file

1. Make active the file window containing the file to be deleted.

2. Highlight the file to be deleted.

3. From the File drop-down menu or FILE COMMANDS menu, select Delete.

4. Select Yes to delete the file.

To delete a group of tagged files

1. Make active the file window containing the files to be deleted.

2. Tag the files.

3. From the Tagged drop-down menu or CTRL FILE COMMANDS menu, select Delete.

4. Select Yes to delete the files.

DOS Command

Purpose

Executes a specified DOS command, and then returns to XTree.

To execute a DOS command without minimizing XTree's memory usage

1. Select eXecute (quick).

2. Enter the DOS command and press Enter.

3. Press Esc to return to XTree.

To increase the memory available for DOS commands

1. Select Alt+eXecute (all memory).

2. Enter the DOS command and press Enter.

3. Press Esc to return to XTree.

Edit File

Purpose

Enables you to make changes to text and binary files.

To edit a file from a directory window

1. From the drop-down File menu, select Edit file (or press Alt+E).

2. Type the name of the file to edit and press Enter.

3. Press Enter to confirm the edit.

4. After making any editing changes, press Esc to access Quick commands, which include Quit without saving and Save file and quit.

To edit a file from a file window

1. Highlight the file to edit.

2. From the drop-down File menu or the FILE COMMANDS menu, select Edit.

3. Press Enter to confirm the edit.

4. After making any editing changes, press Esc to access Quick commands, which include Quit without saving and Save file and quit.

File Display Columns

Purpose

Toggles file display between one, two, or three columns.

To change the file display

From the drop-down Window menu, select File display columns. You also can select Alt+File display from the ALT DIR COMMANDS or ALT FILE COMMANDS menu.

Each time you select the command, the display cycles to the next display column setting.

File Specification

Purpose

Enables you to select a subset of the files on a disk by entering one or more wild card filespecs.

To set the file spec

1. From the drop-down Window menu or the DIR COMMANDS or FILE COMMANDS menu, select File specification.

2. Type up to 28 wild card filespecs and press Enter.

Format Disk

Purpose

Formats a diskette and prepares it for file storage.

To format a diskette

1. Insert the diskette to be formatted into the floppy disk drive.

2. Select Format diskette from the drop-down Volume menu (or press Alt+F2).

3. Specify A or B as the drive to format.

4. Specify High density or Double density for the disk capacity.

5. Press Enter to confirm.

6. At format completion, press Enter to format another diskette or press Esc to return to the menu.

Global

Purpose

Changes the active window to a global file window, which displays all files on all logged disks.

Not included in XTree Easy

To change the active window to a global file window

In the directory window, press G to select Global from the DIR COMMANDS menu or the drop-down Window menu.

Graft Directory

Purpose

Moves complete directory structures and their files.

Not included in XTree Easy

To move a directory and its files

1. In the directory window, highlight the highest level directory to be moved.

2. From the drop-down Directory menu, select **G**raft. You also can select **Alt**+**G**raft from the ALT DIR COMMANDS menu.

3. Highlight the new parent directory and press **Enter**.

4. Select **Y**es to complete the graft or **N**o to cancel the operation.

Help

Purpose

Accesses the XTree on-line help system and provides information about using XTree's features.

To get help

1. Press **F1** or select **H**elp from the XTree drop-down menu.

2. Select the topic for which you want help. To return to XTree, press **Esc**.

Hide/Unhide Directory

Purpose

Hides or unhides directories. Hidden directories do not appear in standard directory displays.

Not included in XTree Easy

To hide or unhide a directory

1. In the directory window, highlight the directory to hide or unhide.

2. From the drop-down Directory menu, select Hide-unhide. You also can select Alt+Hide from the ALT DIR COMMANDS menu.

Invert

Purpose

Toggles the tagged state of files or reverses the filespec.

Not included in XTree Easy

To invert the tagged status of a single file

1. From the file window drop-down Tag menu or the FILE COMMANDS menu, select Invert file tag.

2. Select Tags to invert the tagged status or select File specification to reverse the filespec.

To invert the tagged status of a group of tagged files

1. From the file window drop-down Tag menu, select Invert file tags. You also can select Invert dir files from the directory window drop-down Tag menu, Invert from the DIR COMMANDS menu, or Ctrl+Invert from the CTRL FILE COMMANDS menu.

2. Select Tags to invert the tagged status or File specification to reverse the filespec.

To invert the tagged status of all tagged files on the disk

1. From the directory window drop-down Tag menu, select Invert disk files. You also can select Ctrl+Invert from the CTRL DIR COMMANDS menu.

2. Select Tags to invert the tagged status or File specification to reverse the filespec.

Log Disk/Release Disk

Purpose

Reads the directory and file list for a specified disk or releases a disk's directory and file list from memory.

To log a disk

1. From the drop-down Volume menu or the DIR COMMANDS or FILE COMMANDS menu, select Log disk.

2. Specify the disk to log.

The following steps are not included in XTree Easy

3. From the drop-down Volume menu, select
   Log options. You also can select Alt+Log
   from the ALT DIR COMMANDS or ALT FILE
   COMMANDS menus. Specify log options
   from the following choices:

Option	Function
Branch (or *)	Logs the current directory branch.
Disk drive	Logs the entire disk.
One level (or +)	Logs only the first level under the current directory.
Refresh directory	Relogs only the current directory.
Tree only	Releases all files and logs only directories.

To release a disk's directories and files from memory

1. From the drop-down Volume menu, select
   Release. You also can select Alt+Release
   from the ALT DIR COMMANDS or ALT FILE
   COMMANDS menus.

2. Specify release options from the following
   choices:

Option	Function
Branch	Releases all files and directories in the current branch.
Disk drive	Releases the entire disk.
Files in branch	Keeps the directory tree but releases files.

Make Directory

Purpose

Creates new directories.

To create a new directory

1. In the directory window, highlight the directory that will be the parent directory of the new directory.

2. From the drop-down Directory menu or the DIR COMMANDS menu, select Make.

3. Type the name of the new directory and press Enter.

Merge Tags

Purpose

Combines the file tags in split windows.

Not included in XTree Easy

Reminder

You can only merge tags when the display is split and both windows are file windows.

To combine file tags in split windows.

1. Press F8 to split the display.

2. If both windows are not already file windows, highlight the directory in each directory window that contains the files to tag. Press Enter to move to the file windows.

3. Tag the files you want to tag in each window.

4. Select Merge split tags from the drop-down Tag menu or Ctrl+Merge tags from the CTRL FILE COMMANDS menu. XTree will tag any files in the inactive window that are currently tagged in the active window.

Move File

Purpose

Moves single files or a group of tagged files. Optionally, can move directory structures with files.

To move a single file

1. In the directory window, highlight the directory containing the file and press Enter to make the file window active.

2. Highlight the file you want to move.

3. From the drop-down File menu or the FILE COMMANDS menu, select Move.

4. Type a new name for the file, if you want to rename the file and press Enter. To move the file without changing its name, simply press Enter.

5. Type the name of the destination directory or press F2 to enter point mode and select the destination directory.

6. Press Enter to move the file.

To move a group of tagged files

1. In the directory window, highlight the directory containing the files you want to move and press Enter to make the file window active.

2. Tag the files you want to move.

3. From the drop-down Tagged menu, select Move. You also can select Ctrl+Move from the CTRL FILE COMMANDS menu.

4. Type a new wild card name for the files and press Enter. To move the files without changing their names, simply press Enter.

5. Type the name of the destination directory or press F2 to enter point mode and select the destination directory.

6. Select Yes to overwrite existing files automatically. Select No to be prompted before existing files are overwritten.

7. Press Enter to move the files.

To move related directory structures along with the tagged files

1. In the directory window, highlight the directory that contains the files you want to move and press Enter to make the file window active.

2. Tag the files you want to move.

3. From the drop-down Tagged menu, select Move with paths. You also can select Alt+Move from the ALT FILE COMMANDS menu.

4. Type a new wild card name for the files and press Enter. To move the files without changing their names, simply press Enter.

5. Type the name of the destination directory or press F2 to enter point mode and select the destination directory.

6. Select Yes to overwrite existing files automatically. Select No to be prompted before XTree overwrites existing files.

7. Press Enter to move the files.

Name Disk

Purpose

Adds or changes the volume name of a disk. Enables you to keep track of your diskette files more efficiently.

To add or change the volume name of a disk

1. Make the directory window active.

2. If the disk you want to name is not the current disk, log the disk you want to name. If the disk is currently logged, use < or > to switch to the proper disk.

3. From the drop-down Volume menu, select Name. You also can select Volume from the DIR COMMANDS menu.

4. Type the new name and press Enter.

New date

Purpose

Changes the file date and time for a single file or a group of tagged files.

Not included in XTree Easy

To change a single file

1. In the directory window, highlight the directory that contains the file you want to change and press Enter to make the file window active.

2. Highlight the file you want to change.

3. From the drop-down File menu or the FILE COMMANDS menu, select New date.

4. Type a new date and time for the file and press Enter. To change the date and time to the current system clock setting, simply press Enter.

To change a group of tagged files

1. In the directory window, highlight the directory containing the files and press Enter to make the file window active.

2. Tag the files you want to change.

3. From the drop-down Tagged menu, select New date. You also can select Ctrl+New date from the CTRL FILE COMMANDS menu.

4. Type a new date and time for the files and press Enter. To change the dates and times to the current system clock setting, simply press Enter.

Oops!

Purpose

Recovers files deleted in error.

Not included in XTree Easy

To recover a file

1. In the directory window, highlight the directory containing the deleted file.

2. From the DIR commands menu or the drop-down File menu, select the Oops! command.

3. Highlight the first file to recover.

4. Select Undelete.

5. Type the file name and press Enter.

Note

Begin by undeleting files marked with .**. or you will be unable to recover them after undeleting other files.

Open Archive

Purpose

Opens an archive file and allows you to manage the files contained in the archive.

Not included in XTree Easy

To open an archive file

1. In the directory window, highlight the directory containing the archive file.

2. Press Enter to move to the file window.

3. Highlight the archive file.

4. Press Alt+F5 to open the archive file.

5. Select an option from the ZIP FILE COMMANDS menu:

Option	Function
Delete	Deletes the highlighted file from the archive.
Extract	Extracts the highlighted file from the archive.
Filespec	Determines which files contained in the archive will appear.
Print	Prints the contents of the highlighted file.
Tag	Tags the highlighted file.
Untag	Untags the highlighted file.
View	Views the contents of the highlighted file.

Open File

Purpose

Executes an application program when you select a data file that is associated with the application. Enables you to select the file you want to use rather than select the application program and then load the data file.

Not included in XTree Easy

Reminder

Before using the **O**pen (quick) or Open (all memory) commands, create a batch file in the XTree program directory that starts the application program and passes the name of the data file to the program. The batch file must be named using the extension of the associated data files as its name.

To open a file and the associated application program

1. In the directory window, highlight the directory containing the file and press Enter to make the file window active.

2. Highlight the file that you want to open.

3. From the drop-down File menu or the FILE COMMANDS menu, select Open (quick).

   You also can select Open (all memory) from the drop-down File menu or Alt+Open from the ALT FILE COMMANDS menu. These options open the file and its associated application program and reduce XTree's resident memory size. More memory then is available for the application program.

Note

Some application programs, such as 1-2-3, do not accept a data file name as a command line argument. These programs do not open the highlighted data file and might produce an error message when used with the Open (quick) or Open (all memory) commands.

Partial Untag

Purpose

Untags files that were already operated upon by the last tagged file command. This feature is used when the command is interrupted prior to completion.

Not included in XTree Easy

To untag files that were already operated upon

1. Remain in the file window that was active when the tagged file command was interrupted prior to completion.

2. From the drop-down Tag menu or the CTRL FILE COMMANDS menu, press Ctrl+F8 to select Partial untag. XTree untags the files already operated upon by the interrupted tagged file command. No further confirmation step is included.

Print

Purpose

Prints a catalog of files, a listing of path names, the directory tree, or the contents of selected text files.

To print items in XTree

1. Tag the files you want included in the printing.

2. From the drop-down Volume menu or the DIR COMMANDS menu, select Print.

3. Select Catalog of tagged files, Pathnames, or Tree—depending on what you want to print.

4. Enter the number of lines to print per page and press Enter. To accept the default, just press Enter.

To print the contents of a single file

1. In the directory window, highlight the directory containing the file and press Enter to make the file window active.

2. Highlight the file to print.

3. From the drop-down File menu or the FILE COMMANDS menu, Select Print.

4. Enter the number of lines to print per page and press Enter. To accept the default, just press Enter.

___

To print the contents of a group of tagged files

1. In the directory window, highlight the directory containing the files and press Enter to make the file window active.

2. Tag the files to print.

3. From the drop-down Tagged menu, select Print. You also can press Ctrl+P from the CTRL FILE COMMANDS menu.

4. Enter the number of lines to print on the page and press Enter. To accept the default, just press Enter.

___

Note

When selecting files to print, select text files only. Printing other types of files, such as program files, might result in unexpected characters in the printout.

Quit XTree

___

Purpose

Exits XTree and returns to the DOS prompt.

To exit XTree

Select Quit to exit XTree and return to DOS. (You select Quit from the FILE COMMANDS, DIR COMMANDS, or drop-down XTree menus.) The directory that was current when you started XTree is the current directory.

Select Alt+Quit to exit XTree and return to the currently highlighted XTree directory. (You select Alt+Quit from the ALT FILE COMMANDS, ALT DIR COMMANDS, or drop-down XTree menus.)

Relog Directory

Purpose

Refreshes the file list for the highlighted directory.

To refresh the file list

1. In the directory window, highlight the directory to relog.

2. From the drop-down Directory menu, select Relog. You also can press Alt+F3 from the ALT DIR COMMANDS menu.

Rename Directory

Purpose

Changes the name of a directory.

To rename a directory

1. In the directory window, highlight the directory to rename.

2. From the drop-down Directory menu or the DIR COMMANDS menu, select Rename.

3. Type the new name and press Enter.

Search

Purpose

Searches all tagged files for a specified text string.

Not included in XTree Easy

To search tagged files for a specific text string

1. In the directory window, highlight the directory containing the files to search.

2. Press Enter to move to the file window.

3. Tag the files you want to search.

4. From the CTRL FILE COMMANDS or the drop-down Tagged menu, press Ctrl+S to select Search.

5. At the Search all tagged files for text: prompt, type the text string you want to find in the tagged files and press Enter. XTree untags any files that do not contain the text string.

Showall

Purpose

Changes the active window to a showall file window. This window displays all files on the current disk.

To change the active window to a showall file window

Begin in the directory window. From the DIR COMMANDS menu, press **S** to select **S**howall. You also can select Disk files (**S**howall) from the drop-down Window menu.

Sort Criteria

Purpose

Determines the order in which files appear in the file windows.

To sort files

1. From the drop-down Window menu, select **S**ort criteria. You also can select **Alt+S**ort criteria from the ALT DIR COMMANDS or ALT FILE COMMANDS menu.

2. Select **O**rder to toggle between ascending or descending sort order.

3. Select **P**ath to specify whether files in branch, showall, and global windows should be sorted by directory.

4. Select Name, Ext, Date & Time, Size, or Unsorted to change the sort order.

Split On/Off

Purpose

Toggles between displaying a split display or an unsplit display. A split display can display two directory windows, two file windows, or a combination of a directory window and a file window.

Not included in XTree Easy

To split a display

From the drop-down Window menu or the DIR COMMANDS or FILE COMMANDS menu, select Split on/off.

Statistics

Purpose

Displays the extended disk statistics window, which displays more information about the current disk.

To display statistics

1. From the drop-down Volume menu, select Statistics. You also can press ?.

2. Press Enter or Esc to return to XTree.

Switch to Disk

Purpose

Displays the directories and files on a specified disk.

Not included in XTree Easy

To switch disks

1. From the drop-down Volume menu, select Switch to disk. You also can select Ctrl+Log disk from the CTRL DIR COMMANDS or CTRL FILE COMMANDS menu.

2. Select the disk to switch to.

Tag Files

Purpose

Tags files to indicate which files should be affected by XTree's tagged file commands.

To tag individual files one at a time

1. In the directory window, highlight the directory containing the files to tag and press Enter.

2. Highlight the file to tag and select Tag from the FILE COMMANDS menu or File from the drop-down Tag menu.

To tag all files in a specified directory

1. In the directory window, highlight the directory containing the files to tag.

2. From the DIR COMMANDS menu, select Tag. You also can select Directory files from the drop-down Tag menu.

Or

1. Make the file window active.

2. From the drop-down Tag menu, select All in window. You also can select Ctrl+Tag from the CTRL FILE COMMANDS menu.

To tag all files in a directory branch

1. In the directory window, select the highest level directory to be tagged.

2. From the DIR COMMANDS or drop-down Window menu, select Branch.

3. From the drop-down Tag menu, Select All in window. You also can select Ctrl+Tag from the CTRL FILE COMMANDS menu.

To tag all files on a disk

1. Make a directory window active.

2. From the drop-down Tag menu, select All disk files. You also can select Ctrl+Tag from the CTRL DIR COMMANDS menu.

Or

1. Make the showall window active.

2. From the drop-down Tag menu, select All in window. You also can select Ctrl+Tag from the CTRL FILE COMMANDS menu.

To tag all files on all logged disks

1. Make a global window active.

2. From the drop-down Tag menu, select All in window. You also can select Ctrl+Tag from the CTRL FILE COMMANDS menu.

To tag based on filespec

1. Select Filespec before you select any of the tagging commands.

2. Enter the new filespec.

3. Tag files.

To tag all files in a file window, based on file attributes

1. Make the small, expanded, branch, showall, or global file window active.

2. From the drop-down Tag menu, select All by attributes. You also can select Alt+Tag from the ALT FILE COMMANDS menu.

3. Type the file attributes to use for tagging and press Enter.

To tag all files on a disk based on file attributes

1. Make the directory window active.

2. From the drop-down Tag menu, select All by attributes. You also can select Alt+Tag from the ALT DIR COMMANDS menu.

3. Type the file attributes to use for tagging and press Enter.

Untag files

Purpose

Removes file tags to prevent tagged file commands from affecting selected files.

To untag individual files one at a time

1. In the directory window, highlight the directory containing the files to untag and press Enter.

2. Highlight the file to untag and select Untag from the FILE COMMANDS menu. You also can select File from the untag section of the drop-down Tag menu.

To untag all files in a specified directory

In the directory window, highlight the directory. Then select Untag from the DIR COMMANDS menu or Directory files from the untag section of the drop-down Tag menu.

Or

1. Make the file window active.

2. From the untag section of the drop-down Tag menu, select All in window. You also can select Ctrl+Untag from the CTRL FILE COMMANDS menu.

To untag all files in a directory branch

1. In the directory window, select the highest level directory to be tagged.

2. Select Branch.

3. From the untag section of the drop-down Tag menu, select All in window. You also can select Ctrl+Untag from the CTRL FILE COMMANDS menu.

To untag all files on a disk

1. Make a directory window active.

2. From the untag section of the drop-down Tag menu, select All disk files. You also can select Ctrl+Untag from the CTRL DIR COMMANDS menu.

Or

1. Make the showall window active.

2. From the untag section of the drop-down Tag menu, select All in window. You also can select Ctrl+Untag from the CTRL FILE COMMANDS menu.

To untag all files on all logged disks

1. Make a global window active.

2. From the untag section of the drop-down Tag menu, select All in window. You also can select Ctrl+Untag from the CTRL FILE COMMANDS menu.

To untag files based on filespec

1. Select Filespec before you select any of the untagging commands.

2. Enter the new filespec.

3. Untag files.

To untag all files in a file window based on file attributes

1. Make the small, expanded, branch, showall, or global file window active.

2. From the untag section of the drop-down Tag menu, select All by attributes. You also can select Alt+Untag from the ALT FILE COMMANDS menu.

3. Type the file attributes to use for untagging and press Enter.

To untag all files on a disk based on file attributes

1. Make the directory window active.

2. From the untag section of the drop-down Tag menu, select All by attributes. You also can select Alt+Untag from the ALT DIR COMMANDS menu.

3. Type the file attributes to use for untagging and press Enter.

Video Mode

Purpose

Toggles between displaying 25 lines and 43 lines (EGA) or 51 lines (VGA).

To change the video mode

From the drop-down Window menu, select Video mode. You also can press Alt+F9 from the ALT DIR COMMANDS menu.

View

Purpose

Displays file contents.

To view a single file

1. Highlight the file.

2. From the file window drop-down File menu or the FILE COMMANDS menu, select View.

3. Press Esc to return to the file window.

Not included in XTree Easy

To view a group of tagged files

1. Tag the files to be viewed.

2. From the file window drop-down Tagged menu, select View. You also can select Ctrl+View from the CTRL FILE COMMANDS menu.

3. Select Next tagged file to view the next tagged file or press Esc to return to the file window.

Volume

Purpose

Changes the volume label (name) of the current disk.

To change the volume label of the current disk

1. Make certain that the directory window is active. Press Enter once or twice, if necessary, to change to the directory window.

2. From the DIR COMMANDS menu, select Volume. You also can select Name from the drop-down Volume menu.

3. At the CHANGE DISK VOLUME NAME: to: prompt, type a new name for the disk and press Enter. To keep the current name in place, just press Enter.

Wash Deleted Space

Purpose

Prevents deleted files from being recovered.

Not included in XTree Easy

To prevent deleted files from being recovered

1. From the directory window drop-down Volume menu, select **W**ash deleted space. You also can press **Alt+W** from the ALT DIR COMMANDS menu.

2. Press **F2** to toggle between a single-pass overwrite or a six-pass overwrite.

3. Press **Enter** to overwrite the deleted files on the disk.

Zip

Purpose

Compresses tagged files and adds them to an archive file.

To compress files

Not included in XTree Easy

1. Tag the files to be archived.

2. From the file window drop-down Tagged menu, select **Z**ip. You also can press **Ctrl+F5** from the CTRL FILE COMMANDS menu.

3. Type the name of the archive file. If you want, you can include an EXE extension to create a self-extracting archive file.

4. Select archive options:

Option	Function
Paths	Specifies whether directory paths, or only file names, should be stored.
Encryption	Specifies if the archive should be password-protected.
Method	Specifies whether to add, freshen, or update the archive.
Speed/size	Specifies whether to use the maximum speed or maximum compression.

5. Press Enter to archive the files.

Installing XTree

XTree uses an installation program that makes installing XTree on your hard disk easy. You must use the installation program because XTree's files are compressed and must be expanded before you can use XTree. The installation program also installs the file viewers you select, builds an application menu if requested, and can modify your AUTOEXEC.BAT file so that XTree can start automatically whenever you use your PC.

NOTE The following sections assume that you will be installing XTree using drive A. You also can use drive B to install XTree— which might be necessary if your XTree program disks are the correct size to fit drive B, not drive A. If you are using drive B instead of drive A, simply substitute B whenever the instructions indicate A.

XTree is supplied on three 3 1/2-inch or six 5 1/4-inch disks. During the installation, the screen prompts you when a different disk is needed. Be sure that you insert the proper disk into the drive before pressing Enter or clicking the OK button.

To begin installing XTree, follow these steps:

1. Turn on the power to your PC. When you see the DOS prompt (usually C:\> or something similar) continue to step 2.

2. Insert Disk 1 into drive A and, if you are installing from 5 1/4-inch disks, close the drive handle.

3. Type A: to make the A drive the current drive.

4. Type INSTALL to execute the installation program.

5. Press Enter or click the OK button to continue.

The installation program gives you four options:

Option	Function
Install XTree Gold 2.5 program files	Installs XTree.
Create Applications Menu	Tells XTree to search your hard disk for program files and to create an applications menu for easy execution of your programs.
Install Formatted Viewers	Installs XTree formatted file viewers so that you can view spreadsheet, database, word processing, archive, and graphics files in their native format.
Modify AUTO-EXEC.BAT file	Tells the installation program to modify your AUTOEXEC.BAT file so that XTree starts automatically. Your existing AUTOEXEC.BAT file is renamed as AUTOEXEC.SAV.

6. To change any default selections, press the Tab key to highlight the selection, and then press the space bar to toggle the setting. With a mouse, simply point to the selection and click the left mouse button.

7. To accept the default options (or your selections, if you have made any changes), press Enter or click the OK button.

Next you must register your copy of XTree using the serial number on your registration card. Your name and the serial number are added permanently to your copy of the program, so enter them carefully.

After typing your name, press the Tab key to move to the Company name field. Entering data in this field is optional. Press Tab to move to the Serial number field. Enter the serial number from your registration card and press Enter or click the OK button.

XTree can display many different types of files in their native format. You can, for example, select a Lotus 1-2-3 file and view it as it would appear in worksheet format. XTree uses viewers to display files in their native formats. The next screen lets you install all viewers or select the specific viewers you want. Unless you are short of disk space, accept the default of installing all viewers so that you can display the largest variety of files—even if you do not own the program that created the files.

Press Enter or click the OK button to continue.

XTree attempts to determine the type of display you have installed. Usually, it makes the correct selection, but you are given the option of changing the screen type, if necessary. Unless you are certain that XTree has selected the incorrect type of display, simply press Enter or click the OK button to continue. To change the selection, use the arrow keys or mouse pointer to select the correct display.

The install program begins installing your selections. You are prompted when you need to insert another diskette. Watch the prompts carefully—depending on your selections, some disks might not be required.

After the installation is complete, store the XTree program disks in a safe place. You will need them if you want to reinstall XTree or install additional options. XTree is now ready to use, and you can start it by typing:

> **XTGOLD** (if you have XTreeGold)

or

> **XTREE** (if you have XTree Easy)

> **NOTE** XTree uses your existing mouse driver. If you want to use a mouse with XTree, you must load the driver before starting XTree. Mouse drivers are normally loaded by placing a command line in CONFIG.SYS or AUTOEXEC.BAT. See the documentation that came with your mouse for information on installing the mouse.

Cross-Reference to Older XTree Versions

I f you use a version of XTree that is older than those that this book primarily covers, you might be finding yourself confused and bewildered by many of the features and functions listed. XTree, like any good product, has evolved considerably in the years since its introduction. Many new features have been added and, in some cases, the methods for performing common functions have been changed. This appendix provides information on those changes. This appendix does not, however, detail every minor change in XTree's history.

Function Key Changes

Originally, XTree used the function keys much differently than described in this book. The following is a list of function keys in XTree before XTreePro:

Key	Function
F1	Quits XTree and returns you to DOS.
F2	Accesses the help system.
F3	Cancels an operation.
F4	Removes the menu display.
F5	Keeps the filespec when you log a new disk.
F10	Toggles the screen between displaying the Alt menu and the standard menu.

XTreePro uses the following function keys differently than described in this book:

Key(s)	Function
Alt+F2	This option not available for formatting a diskette.
F5 & F6	Control of directory display not available.
Alt+F8	Partial Untag not available.
F9	Toggles the screen between displaying the Ctrl menu and the standard menu.
F10	Toggles the screen between displaying the Alt menu and the standard menu.
Alt+F10	Direct access to configuration not available.

XTreePro Gold uses the following function keys differently than described in this book:

Key(s)	Function
Alt+F8	Partial Untag not available.
F10	Accesses the quick reference help system.
Alt+F10	Direct access to configuration not available.

Features Added in XTreePro

XTreePro added several of the features described in this book, including

- The Alt+X command to minimize XTree's memory usage when executing DOS programs or commands

- The 1Word text editor to allow editing of text files from within XTree

- The capability to enter four filespec entries

- The capability to log more than one disk at a time

- The global file window

- Ascending, descending, and unsorted file display sort options

Features Added in XTreePro Gold

XTreePro Gold features include

- The application menu

- The Graft, New date, Prune, Wash disk, and Search commands

- The Alt+H command for hiding

- Optional specification of an alternate text editor if you prefer a different text editor than 1Word

- Up to 16 arguments are permitted for the filespec

- The Invert and Ctrl+Invert commands to invert filespecs and file tags

- Mouse support
- Split window displays
- The extended statistics window
- File tagging using file attributes
- Viewing groups of tagged files
- The autoview window
- File archiving

Features Added in XTreeGold

The following XTreeGold features are not available in any older versions of XTree:

- Use of < and > keys to switch between logged drives
- The branch file window
- The Compare command
- Drop-down menus
- The capability to move files and directories to another disk
- The Oops! command for recovering deleted files
- Formatted file viewers, which permit viewing different types of files in their native formats
- The option to build the application menu automatically during installation

INDEX